RIDING
REFLECTIONS

BY PIERO SANTINI

(CAPTAIN ITALIAN CAVALRY RESERVE)

WITH A FOREWORD

BY LIDA L. FLEITMANN

(MRS. J. VAN S. BLOODGOOD, EX M.F.H.)

ILLUSTRATIONS BY
VINCENT FANE HANDLEY

NEW YORK · THE DERRYDALE PRESS

The birth of the forward seat. Captain Caprilli in 1904

PLATE I

TO

THE FRIEND

WHO KNOWS IT BY HEART

PREFACE

THAT practice makes perfect is undoubtedly true, but it would be more accurate to say that intelligent practice makes perfect, for the mechanical repetition of the same acts not only fails to bring us nearer completeness but is rather more apt to confirm us in our original defects.

To the question whether "So-and-so" is a good horseman the answer often is: "Oh, of course; he has ridden all his life." My mental comment to such a reply is that So-and-so may have ridden badly all his life, for by the same token we would logically have to conclude that a man is bound to be a good doctor, a good lawyer or a good cook merely because he has for years followed these particular callings — whereas we know from bitter experience that the doctor, the lawyer and the cook may have exercised their respective professions killing patients, losing cases and distributing indigestion "all their lives."

It is this prevailing attitude of superficiality among amateur horsemen that has tempted me to write the following pages; by amateurs I mean civilians, for in our day all armies of any importance have well organised cavalry schools with highly competent instructors who have made equitation their life study, and whose Governments, of recent years, have facilitated the acquirement of the necessary technique by sending representatives to other countries to widen their horizon by first-hand knowledge. The "regular" officer of the mounted arms can therefore be called a professional, only in the sense, of course, that everything appertaining to riding forms that integral part of his calling to which more and deeper attention is given every day. In England (Weedon) and in Italy such training includes even hunting; in the latter country this branch of horsemanship is obligatory for the pupils of the Cavalry School in the second and complementary stage of instruction which takes place at Tor di Quinto (Rome).

The civilian, on the other hand, in countries where compulsory military service does not exist, is generally an unalloyed dilettante for he rarely has the opportunity for systematic and thorough instruction. If Italy, for example, possesses among her sportsmen so large a percentage of good horsemen, this is indisputably due to the fact that Italians of a certain social category generally do their military service in the mounted arms: cavalry or field- or horse-artillery. Furthermore a large number of our hunting and racing men are ex-officers of the regular army who often have many years of service to their credit plus the very severe and complete Cavalry School training as subalterns. From the non-commissioned officers and from the ranks we draw riding teachers, huntsmen, whippers-in and grooms, all of which contributes to placing us in an enviable position where horsemanship and horsemastership are concerned.

Horsemen can be divided into three categories:

First: "Regular" officers and non-commissioned officers of the mounted arms in active service or of the reserve.

Second: Civilians who have done compulsory military service in the mounted arms.

Third: Civilians with no military service to their credit.

The first category, of course, ranks highest in efficiency, for its members enjoy or have enjoyed all possible advantages, including (for all cavalry officers and a certain number of picked officers and non-commissioned officers of all mounted arms) cavalry school instruction. The second class comes next in quality for, although not having had the advantages of Cavalry School training, contact with the "regulars" and with an enormous variety of horses during the many months of compulsory service added to the duties of its various phases, go far to develop any innate ability the recruit may originally possess. The third class constitutes the mass of the amateur world; its members, which naturally include the weaker sex, do what they can according to their aptitudes, individual circumstances and environment: some are bad, some are good, a few excellent — the last generally because they have had the good fortune to obtain proper training from a relative or friend graduated from a cavalry school. Such training is recognizable at a glance as I have found on more than one occasion. *

To the onlooker the show ring offers an unlimited field for the study of every phase of horsemanship — jumping in particular — and much can be observed and learnt from a comfortable seat by the rails. I have had many opportunities and fully profited by them, especially of late; a physical disability having temporarily placed me *à pied*, I was reduced to the rôle of spectator even at hunts and drags — a good way of taking in both detail and ensemble of the proceedings. When riding to hounds ourselves we have neither the detachment nor the desire to note how our fellow sportsmen are faring and we do not particularly care so long as their actions have no direct bearing on our own amusement; the opportunities for observation,

* Mrs John Tupper Cole, whom I had the pleasure of seeing at a horse show on Long Island in the summer of 1931 — but not, unfortunately, over jumps — is a case in point

iv.

however, of a disabled hunting man at the meet, or following hounds with motor car and field glasses are on the contrary unlimited.

The notes I made mentally in the light of many years' experience of military and "horsey" civilian communities, I have attempted to embody in the following pages which, I hasten to add, in no sense constitute a text book. If we run our eye over the bookshelves of forty years or so ago, we will find that it was then the fashion to entitle books "All about Chemistry" or "All about Astronomy" or knitting or tiddley winks. One cannot possibly write "all about" even backgammon in one or even twenty volumes and it is a proof of the modesty born of wisdom that today no one thinks of writing "all about" anything. This book therefore is decidedly *not* all about riding, but an unpretentious collection of suggestions without much rhyme but, I trust, not altogether without reason. If it appears incomplete I might almost say that it is purposely so, for all I have attempted is to jot down certain reflections — based on principles of equitation that have by now stood the test of years — for the correction of current defects and misconceptions regarding riding position in those past the tyro stage and therefore not in need of primary instruction.

In connection with what I expound I lay claim to at least one qualification. I am old enough to have ridden in two ways: already in my twenties when the new theories were evolved, I was obliged to change my seat very radically from the "lean back" to the "forward" position; thanks to excellent instruction and the very evident logic of fresh ideas, the transition was made, almost without effort, in a remarkably short time. I mention this so that the reader may realize that my defence of modern methods accurately conceived is not chauvinistic but the result of unbiased observation and practical experience of widely differing schools.

P. Santini.

Rome, July, 1932.

CONTENTS

LIST OF ILLUSTRATIONS

ix

LIST OF ILLUSTRATIONS

LIST OF ILLUSTRATIONS

FOREWORD

DURING the past decade we have almost been surfeited with books by horsemen of various nationalities, but the country which has contributed a world-wide revolutionizing principle of equitation has hitherto unfortunately remained silent.

Like most Americans I was brought up to believe that from a horsey point of view everything Anglo-Saxon was the best. From England and Ireland came the finest horses, saddles, grooms, and above all, riders — while these countries were also the Mecca of all hunting people.

Foreign officers competing at Olympia and Madison Square Garden won our reluctant — but patronizing — admiration, and we felt convinced that they were mere "trick" riders on "trick" horses.

It was not until I had spent many winters in Europe that I realized that the Italians have little to learn in things equestrian; that the methods, moreover,

which enabled them to take any kind of animal —
thoroughbred, Sardinian pony or ex-dray-horse —
and make it jump phenomenal obstacles to perfection,
were equally applicable to the hunting field, and that
these same men and horses crossed a country as fast
and as stiff as any in the British Isles or America.

Captain Santini's book gives us for the first time
some of these principles in print. Seldom put into
black and white even in Italian, they have never accurately been expressed in English. The book is therefore outstanding in what it has to contribute.

The author is unusually well qualified for the work:
in addition to his thorough command of the English
language, which has rendered a translation — with all
its attendant misconceptions — unnecessary, his cos-
mopolitan experience gives him a viewpoint of breadth
and impartiality. He has approached the subject and
written about it with much originality, and even to
those of us who have read almost everything that has
appeared in print about horses this book will stand
out as refreshingly new both in its content and its
treatment.

In wishing it the success it deserves I cannot say
more than that personally — as one who has had a
wide and varied experience of hunting, showing, and
judging both horses and horsemen — to dissect riding
with the meticulous eye of its author was a revelation.

Lida L. Fleitmann.

(Mrs. J. Van S. Bloodgood, ex-M.F.H.)

The Saumur seat

The Italian seat

The Italian seat

CHAPTER I

"SCHOOLS" AND THE FORWARD SEAT

THE proportion of people who still ride 'cross country and over jumps sitting back and with the straight leg of the 'nineties is daily diminishing, for the much discussed forward seat has come to stay, and even if all its advocates do not by any means interpret it correctly, the fact that even in its most hybrid forms it has spread the world over in the teeth of bitter opposition on the part of the conservative "diehards" conclusively proves the soundness of its underlying idea. It was created thirty-four years ago by an Italian, whose name, like that of many another inventor of good and useful things, is barely known outside his own country.

Captain Federico Caprilli was a cavalry officer who dedicated ten years (1897 to 1907) of his short life, to revolutionizing the system of horsemanship then prevalent and rapidly replacing it in Italy by a rational method of his own, the result of indefatigable work and study.

In the first years of its appearance outside the country of its birth, — 1908 and immediately following, — "Italian seat" was, to be sure, a current expression, but as time wore on and people became familiar with the new position, the original designation seemed to wear itself threadbare and was replaced by "forward seat" — for the Italian manner was so rapidly permeating the riding world that its source was soon lost sight of. The Italian military authorities had not only made no effort to monopolize the system for the exclusive benefit of our army, but had on the contrary with sporting generosity opened the doors of the Cavalry School to officers of all nations. Since 1907 — with the exception of the war period — every year has seen a considerable number of foreign pupils at the Cavalry School, and if English, Americans, Russians, Japanese, Swedes, Swiss, Poles, Argentines, Roumanians, Bulgarians, etc., have successfully adopted the "new" seat and even triumphed in international competitions, the reason is traceable in every instance to direct Italian instruction or indirect Italian influence. To quote but two examples covering widely differing periods, mention need only be made of the Russian Army Team, led by Captain Paul Rodzanko, which made such a brilliant showing before the war at Olympia, and the

United States Army Team which rode so perfectly over the jumps of the International Course at Madison Square Garden in 1931. Both Captain — now Colonel — Rodzanko and Major Chamberlin are graduates of the Italian Cavalry School (Pinerolo and Tor di Quinto).

When the lively and energetic Lieutenant Caprilli was recalled from the small garrison in the South of Italy where he had been sent to cool his heels and his juvenile exuberance after a somewhat hectic début in Turin, the method which was to make him famous was already clear in his mind. In his exile, owing to his astonishing success in steeplechases and in jumping competitions, he had caught the eye of an intelligent superior officer, and it was thanks to the faith he had succeeded in inspiring in the latter that the young officer — who seems to have had but few partisans of his method at the time — was allowed to demonstrate, to a special committee nominated for the purpose, the practical results of his theories. He presented to the critical and not altogether benevolent eye of his superiors a troop he had been instructing for four months; the result was a veritable triumph, and in 1904 we find Caprilli installed at Pinerolo with carte blanche as to the instruction of the yearly batch of young subaltern pupils.

[3]

Such was the dawn of what might be called the contemporary era of riding.

Caprilli was not much given to writing and the little he did put on paper deals more with the rider's mental attitude towards the horse*—which might be described as one of gentle persuasion as opposed to the forcible methods then in vogue — than with the rider's actual position as he conceived it. The result has been that, never really having compiled an exhaustive treatise on every detail of his method, most of his principles have been handed down, mainly by word of mouth, to succeeding generations of Italian Cavalry instructors. This has prevented strict standardization and, outside of the Italian Cavalry, has led to a certain misleading elasticity of interpretation which Caprilli's written word would have done much to keep within bounds.

At the time of Caprilli's appearance on the scene of Pinerolo, horsemanship there, as everywhere else in the world, was based on severe bits and on leaning back at jumps with the feet thrust forward in such a way that the rider was practically dependent on the reins for keeping his seat; and on that most illogical of all theories, "lifting" the horse over the jump by violently jerking his head up — practices which Caprilli condemned as causing discomfort and pain to the horse and consequently disgusting him with his work.

* *Principi di Equitazione di Campagna,* Ten F Caprilli, 1901

[4]

Caprilli entirely suppressed the prevailing methods and based his own on the principle that a horse should be interfered with as little as possible and that, although continually under the rider's control (he was the sworn enemy of the loose rein), he should move with the freedom and natural balance of a riderless animal — this to apply to all contingencies and not to jumping alone, for the forward seat does not consist, as the amateur is apt to believe, in a *jumping formula*, but should be understood as a complete and distinct method of equitation.

France, Germany and Belgium are among the few European nations who have abstained from sending representatives to the Italian Cavalry School.

There is justification for the first named because it has traditions of its own of which it is patriotically jealous. Saumur still teaches the time-honored *haute école* which Pinerolo inherited from Austria but long since abandoned, and the French seat, originally radically different from the Italian, was undoubtedly based on theories of its own which until very recently Saumur uncompromisingly upheld.

If the French "school" has been till now so independent as to be worthy of the name, the same cannot be said for the German or the Belgian. Although no officers from either of these armies have ever been detailed to Italy, this has not enabled them to resist the all-pervading Italian influence.

A not too satisfying version of the "Italian" seat allowed Germany — the most recent arrival in international arenas — to beat us at our own game in Rome in 1931 when we lost to her the same Mussolini Gold Cup we had successfully defended against France two years before in a famous duel between Captain Bizard on *Pantin* and Major Bettoni on *Aladino* — the victory going to the latter by the shortest of margins and after one of the most thrilling exhibitions of two distinct techniques ever witnessed in a show ring. Both riders and horses of the German team of 1931 were open to adverse criticism, but on their next appearance (1932) when they won the second "leg" of the Mussolini Cup, a truly remarkable improvement was noticeable; the type of horse ridden by most of the German officers has caused much discussion and their value outside the show ring will ever remain a matter of dispute, but it is undeniable that with characteristic thoroughness the Germans are rapidly evolving, in both horses and horsemen, qualities which will make them truly formidable rivals, particularly in those jumping classes typical of Italian "Concorsi Ippici" where nothing counts except getting over jumps without actually knocking them down and completing the course within a reasonable time limit.

[6]

In conclusion, few nations of any importance or tradition have not fallen, consciously or unconsciously, under the influence of Italy. Little Austria stands out by obstinately clinging to the florid *manège* schooling inherited from the Spaniards. The French still keep their *haute école* and their typical *dréssage* — though at the time of writing rumour has it that the present Saumur authorities are lending a not unwilling ear to Italian suggestions. England, the most conservative of countries, has sent representatives to Pinerolo and Tor di Quinto, and the results are Weedon and what in England now goes by the name of "Weedon seat." Fort Riley is very near Italy in spite of the 4000 miles that divide them; the pre-war Russian army owed much — certainly the forward seat — to the already mentioned Colonel Rodzanko, for a time instructor to the Irish Free State Cavalry. Other officers of the Czar, who have taken refuge principally in the United States and with admirable adaptability have turned what was once their professional pride, their pleasure and their sport into a means for earning most honourable livings, base their teaching on the Italian idea, in some instances perhaps unconsciously. Practically the whole world has drawn from the same taproot and the military centres of Europe and North and South America are moulding, with ever better results, the amateur civilian element, both male and female. Even

[7]

if the basic principle gets somewhat distorted in pass-
ing from hand to hand the essence of the right spirit
survives, and if better performances both in style, and
ease for horse and man, emerge, a thought is due to the
country of the *real* forward seat.

PLATE 5

Seated; weight on horse's loins

PLATE 6

Seated; tibia and foot at right angles

CHAPTER II

GEOMETRY OF THE FORWARD SEAT

ON SITTING

THE verb "to sit" should be eliminated from our vocabulary where riding is concerned, for the idea it conveys is intrinsically misleading. Were it not for its indecorous connotation the word "perch" would more aptly suggest the position that the rider should assume in what is commonly described as the "forward" seat.

By saying that if the back of the saddle were cut away the modern horseman ought never to notice its absence, we would be giving an extreme but accurate illustration of the only poise which makes the rider elastically one with the horse. In other words he should be well forward in the saddle, with loins bent inwards, and fork close to the pommel, thereby reducing to the least possible fraction contact between buttocks and saddle. If this position is adopted we are immediately

[9]

struck by the impression that a horse can comfortably carry much more than his usual burden, and for obvious reasons; he has the bulk of the rider's weight where he feels it the least, i.e., on the forehand, his propelling apparatus — loins and quarters — free of encumbrance. The advantage of this particular balance can be put to a convincing practical test when hunting horses not up to one's weight; how much more can be got out of them will be a surprise to anyone who has never before ridden properly "forward."

I stress the necessity for lightening the horse's load as much as possible because although people agree in theory they more seldom carry out the idea in practise than is believable, at the back of their heads there being always the ineradicable word "seat;" if the rider allows himself to be dominated by it he may as well forget that forward riding exists and call his own brand something else. Plate 5 is an example of leaning the body forward from the waist without rising from the saddle or bending the loins.

Apart from practical reasons against it, nothing gives a greater impression of lack of style and chic in a horseman than using the saddle as he would the family armchair; although the heel up and toe down defect — of which hereafter — is serious, the sitting down posture and the round back are sins hardly less grievous. (Plate 6.) They are both intimately con-

C
6
5
4
A
3
2
1
B
D

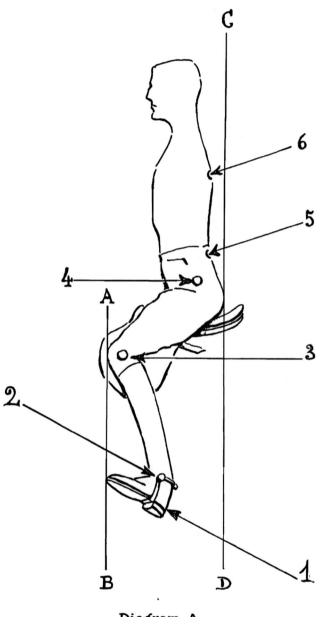

Diagram A

nected with the position of the knee and ankle, for if the ankle, knee and loins are not, singly and collectively, right the whole position is defective.

Diagram A is an effort to explain mechanically, so far as it is possible with pen and paper, the gist of theories difficult to make clear without practical demonstration. Nevertheless I hope that I may succeed in suggesting to the reader's mind how the joints that come into play in riding are employed and the direction in which — at first consciously and later instinctively — the principal component parts of the skeleton should act according to the requirements of pace and jumps.

I have simplified the human anatomy to the profile of a five-jointed marionette without muscle or flesh because both the latter will take care of themselves if we keep in mind the position of the bones and their angles. I use the term "marionette" advisedly, for the style of a finished horseman should in effect resemble the trim-jointed lightness of a harlequin. Although it may seem unfitting to apply the word graceful to anything as wooden as a puppet I find no better adjective to convey that almost brittle impression that an angular, though not stiff, position gives. (Plate 7.) To use a painter's simile, a horseman should present to the eye the simplicity of line characteristic of the early

[13]

Primitives, which is brittle, angular but graceful withal. Any curved effect, sitting down in the saddle, rounded back, etc., is to be carefully avoided, for angles, not curves, will give us that truly workmanlike wiriness by which even the heavyweights will be able to take off a few pounds, not only from their horse's backs, but in the eyes of their friends as well. The heavier we sit the heavier we look — and are.

ON MISCONCEPTIONS

A large number of people have, nowadays, in a sort of incomplete and groping way adopted *a* forward seat, but the fundamental principles of the real thing appear so far to have escaped them — though we may at least be thankful that by attempting at all costs to throw their weight forward over jumps they generally succeed in freeing their horses' heads. The fact nevertheless remains that apart from this step in the right direction the majority carry in their minds a hybrid and disconnected mixture of the old and the comparatively new, the ruling misconception being that the key to perfection consists in shortening the leathers sometimes to an absurd degree, and pitching forward over fences — whereas the principles of the forward seat are barely affected by the length of the leathers, and apply to all paces; in other words they constitute a distinct riding position and complete method, and not

FIGURE 1. *One of the most frequent misconceptions of the forward seat: Toe down, back rounded, loose reins, hands on horse's neck*

simply a convenient way of surmounting obstacles. Plates 8 and 9 respectively walking and at a halt may help to illustrate my meaning. Most defects can be solved by correcting the position of the foot and ankle and consequently that of the knee, for so long as any portion of the landscape, however limited, is visible between knee and saddle — the direct result of the foot being turned down and in, like a toe dancer's doing the time honoured pirouette — just so long will the rider's weight remain uncontrolled. (Figure 1.)

Any man or woman with a normal figure riding astride should not find it difficult to assume the position shown in Diagram A. For most people the hardest part appears to be the flexing of the ankle in such a way as not only to force the heel *down* and the toe *up,* but also the foot *outward* to the point of showing the sole of the boot to the spectator standing on the same level with the horse, — or, to put it otherwise, with the small toe higher than the big toe. (Plates 7, 8 and 9.)

To recapitulate and complete the above points we must keep in mind:

First: That we should never really be *seated* in the saddle and should not reserve what is conventionally known as the "forward" position to the one mad moment when we fling ourselves very much forward over jumps, as is often done with quite unnecessary abandon. (Plate 10.)

Second: That the leathers should be short enough to give the distinct feel of the stirrups and to bring the thigh approximately to the position shown in Diagram A. The angle of the thigh is the least important detail so long as the others are strictly observed, for it depends largely on the conformation of the rider and the length of his thigh bone, the short leather being insufficient — even deleterious — in itself if unaccompanied by the right poise.

Third: That the knee should be kept close to the saddle, a result naturally and *effortlessly* obtained if the heel is *down*, the toe *up* and the foot turned *outwards*. (Plate 11.)

Fourth: That the foot should never go beyond the perpendicular of the knee — in other words, that were a line to be dropped from the knee to the ground, the toe should be *within* this line. (Line A-B, Diagram A.)

From the knee down the position should never vary whatever pace we may be going or whatever obstacles we may be negotiating. Ditto for going down hill, or up, or for refusals, run-outs and similar tragi-comic incidents, the principle being that the knees forced into the saddle by the position of the feet and the flexing of the ankles, act as a *pivot* and give natural grip.

[18]

PLATE 7

Correct position: Standing
Tor di Quinto Cavalry School

PLATE 8

Correct position: Walking
Tor di Quinto Cavalry School

PLATE 9

Correct position

PLATE 10

Exaggerated forward position

Furthermore, the ankle, — and to a lesser degree the knee, — acts as a shock absorber, particularly in landing over a jump, and in fact should at all paces and in all emergencies perform the service of the springs of a car or carriage. Since by these means the knee is prevented from sliding back and forth in the saddle even if the position of the body is deliberately or accidentally altered, the weight of the latter will not be running up and down the horse's back from withers to loins, and the foot, rebelliously pointing earthward, swinging like a pendulum from shoulder to stifle. (Figure 1.)

The commonest and gravest failing of all would-be adepts of the forward seat is, primarily, neglect of the proper functions of the ankle and loins. If we press *in* the loins in the direction of Arrow 5 and press *down* the ankle in the direction of Arrow 2, at the same time raising the foot up and outwards (Arrow 1) keeping the toe behind the perpendicular A-B, we are mechanically forced into a correct position, which is further completed by being so on the fork, that, to use an Italian expression, a sheet of paper could be passed with ease between buttocks and saddle.

ON LEATHERS

At this juncture a word as to stirrup leathers will not come amiss.

In the old days it was customary to adjust the length of one's leathers by laying the tips of one's fingers on the stirrup bar and the bottom of the stirrup in the armpit; in other words the riding length of the stirrup was from finger tip to armpit. This manner of measuring did approximately give the right length with the old seat, although then, as now, the individual conformation of each horse could alter the general rule to the point of a hole or more either way; obviously the rounder ribbed the animal, the longer the leather, so as to compensate the loss of length by greater curve.

For the seat we are considering the same system can be applied as a basis, with the difference that the tip-of-finger-armpit length should be reduced by two or even three holes to obtain the proper riding length of leather which, in the correct position of the leg specified above, gives the foot the purchase necessary to force the knee into close contact with the saddle. The foot should be well home in the stirrup.

Of course the shorter leather will raise the knee completely beyond the flap of an ordinary straight English type of saddle (Figure 2) but as I go on the assumption that such a saddle has at the outset been discarded, this does not apply to the one I deal with under another heading and which is radically different.

[20]

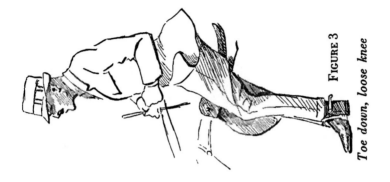

FIGURE 3

Toe down, loose knee

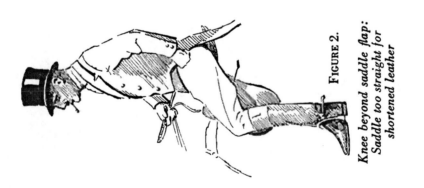

FIGURE 2.

Knee beyond saddle flap:
Saddle too straight for
shortened leather

ON ANGLES

These two points — leathers and saddle — having been established, we can return to the position of that portion of the rider's anatomy comprised of the part between the sole of the foot and the shoulder joint, arms and hands being purposely neglected for the moment clearly to underline their detachment.

To adopt a system of reversion so as to get away from all conventional modes of teaching, the points one should consider are:

> Ankle
> Knee
> Thigh joint
> Loins
> Shoulder blade vertebrae

Practical application will prove that there is method in this madness: it is easier to catch the right position by going, figuratively speaking, from the foot up, than it is, as is usually done, by the downward head-to-foot method.

The following, therefore, is the order in which, were we giving a practical lesson, our eye should travel for the correction of errors:

Heel *down*, toe *up* in the direction of Arrow 1, sole *outwards*.

Ankle joint flexed *downwards* in the direction of Arrow 2, and *inwards*.

Knee *forward* in the direction of Arrow 3.

Hip joint *backwards* in the direction of Arrow 4.

Loins *in* and *down* in the direction of Arrow 5.

Shoulder blades *flat* and vertebrae of shoulder *in*, in the direction of Arrow 6.

From the knee, which should be the *immovable* pivot or hinge of all action, upwards, the body should follow the movements of the horse and be more or less forward according to pace, jumps and emergencies; neither back nor shoulders should be rounded. Furthermore in no case, it must be well understood, should any part of the body, heels included, swing behind the perpendicular C-D, nor the toes beyond A-B, not even going down the steepest inclines (Plates 14 and 46).

To demonstrate geometrically the position with respect to each other of the bones from foot to loins, Diagram A shows that for balance to be correct tibia and foot should *invariably* form acute angles. Thigh and tibia should on principle be approximately at right angles to each other, although in this respect, outside the halt and the walk, the necessity for a certain latitude is evident; in jumping we widen this angle to a greater or lesser degree to bring the body forward, at the same time that the pelvis reduces the right angle it forms with the thigh bone, to an acute angle.

PLATE 11

Good knee position

PLATE 12

A good example of heel down

PLATE 13

The forward seat in the drop. Double bank at Tor di Quinto

PLATE 14

Forward position down steep incline
Slide at Tor di Quinto

ON CONSTRAINT

Much has been said regarding the "constrained" position that the Italian seat entails, and that the foregoing may suggest.

In the Italian army the seat is the same for both officers and troopers, and though the latter use a deeper and heavier type of saddle, the former march, manœuvre, parade and cross a country with their men on the identical saddles and in the identical position that they use when hacking, hunting or showing. The writer has himself covered for weeks his full daily quota of miles, with no material change in the position of loins, knee and ankle described, not only without undue fatigue but in perfect comfort.

If most other physical exercises, notably fencing and golf, demand for their proper accomplishment positions to a certain extent forced, which can only become easy and natural when attitudes evolved by experience and study have mechanically developed certain muscles and tendons which in the ordinary occupations of life do not come into play, why should equitation be an exception? And why should we dismiss continued physical effort in its connection as unnatural, uncomfortable and constrained? The position of the various parts of the body in golf are far from natural or comfortable for the beginner, but they have been evolved by the experience of many to give the

[25]

best results for the particular purposes of that game, just as the "guard" and the "lunge" in fencing have become what they are for the swordsman's objects. No one can say that his first lessons either in golf or fencing were very enjoyable muscularly, or that they did not require a constraint which, later becoming natural, in due time allowed instinctive relaxation without loss of correct position. In riding, as in fencing or golf or any other athletic sport or game, we all know rigidity does not give the best results, but in all of them this constraint disappears the moment our trained body responds without effort or fatigue to the principles our mind has so completely grasped as to turn them into effortless instinct.

ABOVE THE BELT

I have, so far, purposely not dealt in detail with anything but the position from the loins down because arms and hands should be independent of the rest of the body; to emphasize my point by exaggeration I might say that all I have so far written applies to an armless rider. The position I have advocated and which should be preserved at all paces and on all occasions should be capable of being kept with arms crossed, so independent should we be of the reins and any support from bit and mouth. It may seem superfluous and idle to say this because we are all supposed to know that

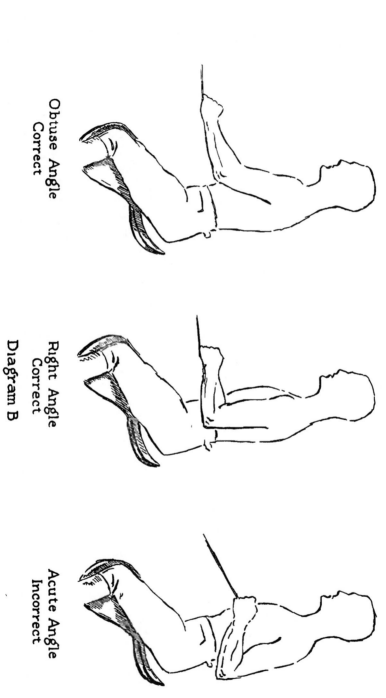

Obtuse Angle
Correct

Right Angle
Correct

Diagram B

Acute Angle
Incorrect

one does not hold on by the reins, but that many —
the majority — do not in actual fact apply the knowledge they think they possess can easily be proved by
referring, as in the case of other riding defects, to the
photographs scattered broadcast by the daily, weekly
and monthly press. The camera is a most inconsiderate
recorder of our shortcomings!

ARMS

Having established what the position should be from
the shoulder down, we can proceed to consider that
part of the horseman's anatomy which might be termed the continuation of the reins and which establishes
direct contact with the horse's head and neck through
the medium of the bit, and influences so greatly what
are conventionally termed "hands" that its functions
to be correct and really efficacious should also be kept
within correct limits.

To apply the same geometric demonstration to the
position of the arms (wrist to shoulder) as has been
used for the lower part of the body (foot to loins) we
have only to reverse the principle, by keeping in mind
that if the latter are to form, with respect to each
other, acute and right angles, the arm and forearm
should on the contrary tend to form right and obtuse
angles. (Diagram B.)

A variety of the acute angle — besides the one shown

in this diagram — is the result of that "knitting" position of the hands — the fists drawn up almost to the chin — which we associate with children's "good hands" classes and which has no *raison d'etre* outside the show ring and remarkably little connection with the "goodness" of hands.

The forearm should always be kept low — on a level with the waist line under ordinary conditions, (right angle of arm and forearm), and the hands below the line of the withers and mane when jumping, (obtuse angle of arm and forearm).

Hands should never be nearer the body than four or five inches — in action very much farther, for our style of equitation excludes reins long enough to allow hands to rest elegantly on the groin or against the waistcoat with elbows stuck out; the latter should rather tend, on the contrary, to converge towards each other as the hands get so forward as to be free of body and ribs.

STRAIGHT LINES

The tendency to form straight lines with foot, tibia and thigh bone and with arm and forearm is to be avoided as the greatest possible error: the results are illustrated to perfection by Plate 18, which shows the jockey in the lead seated *behind* the saddle and with his weight entirely on the horse's loins, a position inevitable if we point the feet forward and throw the body back; furthermore, the arms are straightened out and the reins have been made to slip through the fingers to the very buckle with the laudable intention of not interfering with the horse's head. This object could have been better and more easily attained, by leaning forward and keeping the foot within the knee perpendicular—in other words, by preserving *angles,* the secret of elasticity. The second jockey is doing still worse, for he is pulling his mount's head to him, almost as violently as the jockey on the extreme right of Plate 19.

Positions such as these are the result of a seat which is neither fish, flesh nor fowl, and all too common — may I be permitted to say so — among English steeplechase jockeys, both amateur and professional, who affect leathers almost as short as those of their flat-racing brethren. See, for example, photographs of steeplechasers in the paddock or during the "parade." Short leathers, without the forward poise that must accompany them, are worse than useless, for they cause weight to be shifted still more toward the horse's loins than was even the case with the old fashioned seat, besides rendering the rider dangerously insecure in the saddle.

FINGERS

I use the term "fingers" and not "hands" for the same reason that in the preceding pages I have tried to eradicate from the reader's mind the dominating idea of *sitting* a saddle.

Just as the word "seat" seems to convey a sense of bulk and heaviness which is the antithesis of good horsemanship, so the idea of "hands" when applied to that part of the rider's anatomy directly connected with his mount's most sensitive organ, the mouth, appears to suggest but a fistful of leather. A fist in appearance it must perforce be, for it is only by closing or crooking our fingers that we can hold the reins, but real "hands," that is the two sets of four fingers and two thumbs, should resemble those of a violinist in suppleness and sensibility. I have seen things done by a mere twist of a little finger in the fraction of a second by first-class horsemen that would have taken the whole arm and shoulder — the knees and heels as well — of minor lights to do far less well. Nothing is quicker and stronger if properly employed than the fingers; in the subtler shadings of pace or jumping effort nothing can replace them; but, as for the other finer points of the game, many are called but few are chosen to become Kreislers of the rein, most of us, alas! must remain content with an unassuming place in the orchestra.

It will always be a matter of conjecture what good hands really consist in and to what exact degree they are influenced by seat. That a position in the saddle

[32]

PLATE 15

Compare with Plate 16

PLATE 16

Consistency of position on take-off and landing

Jumping position correct in every detail: Heel down, toe up, foot outward, loins concave, contact perfect

PLATE 17

which allows complete independence of the torso is an invaluable asset is indisputable, but, nevertheless, one sees all around one examples which would almost seem to contradict this theory. For instance, one of the best pair of hands I have ever seen is the envied possession of a friend of mine, the type of hunting man who makes a point of avoiding fences. As he always rides very fast horses and is on intimate personal terms with all the gates in the country, he sees most of the fun at not too great a distance. He has one of the ugliest and loosest seats that has ever come to my notice, but since he never jumps, he never runs the risk of coming off or jabbing his horse in the mouth, or to any extent losing his balance; his seat therefore is of secondary importance for his own particular purposes. His velvet touch permits him to handle in the most surprising manner the kind of neurotic pulling brutes that would give better horsemen most uncomfortable rides. That, just as he cannot jump, he would also be helpless to prevent a "bad actor" from going home without him has no bearing on the fact that in his particular case his hands do not suffer from his poor seat.

In spite of what sporadic instances, such as the above, might lead us to believe, however, I think we may safely assert that for hands to be good *for all purposes* they should go at least with firmness in the saddle.

[33]

It stands to reason that secure poise contributes to lightness of hand for it eliminates the necessity of forever relying on the reins to keep or regain balance; that this is a point in favour of the position I have attempted to analyze, it would be difficult even for its bitterest adversaries to deny.

In this connection, and without wishing in any way to detract from the almost proverbial reputation for light hands women enjoy, we are tempted to ask ourselves whether the firmness of seat the side-saddle naturally engenders is not largely responsible for that particular virtue in women riders we are apt to attribute to more elusive qualities. If we add to it the naturally lighter touch born of lesser strength have we not perhaps revealed the secret of women's "wonderful hands?" Few of them who ride astride, I have observed, possess on an average much better hands than men; this might be explained by the fact that their rounder and less muscular conformation preventing proper contact with the saddle flaps — especially when riding in the old way — action on the reins is more erratic because not so independent of the body, even if "touch" is naturally lighter. Women astride often look very well at a walk, trot, canter or even gallop, but rarely in the more violent exercise of jumping, particularly if all does not go quite smoothly; on the whole, they cut a much better figure in the side saddle, particularly if they apply the "forward" position to it.

To write about hands in the hope of practically benefiting the reader can only be an illusion; all I can attempt is to lighten the accepted conception of what they really are, by transferring the mental picture of the whole to its component parts. Firmness should be amalgamated with velvety softness and extreme sensibility, which, as it forms part of individual temperament, is or is not, and never can be acquired. In fencers the same indescribable quality, as important on the hilt of the sword as it is on the reins, is most aptly described by a French word: *doigtée*.

WRISTS

The fencing simile brings us directly to another part of the human anatomy which has its place — though in a lesser degree — in horsemanship as well.

The wrist plays such an important part in the *haute école* that in its antithesis — the Italian "equitazione naturale" — it is tacitly ignored, not because its use is meant to be suppressed by deliberate rigidity, but rather with the idea that by mentioning it as little as possible — at least in writing — the votaries of old systems will be unconsciously weaned from its excessive use. The wrist, therefore, has fallen — in a simpler method of less florid requirements — to subsidiary rank.

[35]

A free and supple wrist contributes to lightness of hand, but can also when called upon bear with sufficient severity on the horse's mouth as to substitute, up to a certain point, the intrinsically less subtle action of arms and forearms. If, for instance, when galloping we wish to regulate pace without modifying the position of the arms, we can give more or less rein by merely changing the angle of the finger bones either way, by lowering or raising the hand from the hinge of the wrist. (Plates 20, 21, 22 and 23.) This also gives excellent results in jumping, notably in the phases described on pages 52 and 62 when, by this means, we are enabled to regulate contact to the finest shadings without changing the position of any other joint when any more brusque alteration might result in disturbing the horse exactly when his attention should be as little as possible distracted.

One of the many examples of what can be done in this connection came to my notice some years ago, and the artistry of the performance was such that I have never forgotten it. A horseman of world renown whose resources in emergencies and quickness of decision are perhaps unrivalled, was taking part in a jumping competition in which, among other obstacles, was a double composed of post and rails and a big brush fence. Evidently the measurements had been miscalculated, for the space between the two jumps did not allow for the usual two full strides, and the proximity of the second obstacle to the first had caused all previous competitors to knock down the former. When it came to my friend's turn, once over the post and rails, by an almost imperceptible combined movement of the wrists and fingers he shortened his mount's action between landing and take-off by just those few inches necessary to prevent his horse taking off too close to the second obstacle — thereby clearing it brilliantly and making the only clean performance in that class.

The wrist is useful in bringing pullers and borers to reason without excessive and often all too noticeable effort. By dropping our hands to the withers and keeping one wrist rigid while with the other we bring firm and even pressure to bear repeatedly on the horse's mouth by a change of the angle of the hand so that its outer part describes a concentric half circle with the thumb as its fulcrum (Plate 24) many a warm ride can be brought to its senses. In extreme cases — with very powerful horses in high condition, for example — this action can be alternated from left to right and vice versa. To obtain a maximum of power from this movement our shoulder muscles and pectoral muscles should be deliberately brought into play, and the snaffle reins kept under the little finger; obviously the larger the arc of the circle described by the rein finger the greater the leverage on the horse's bars.

ON PERFECTION

In no branch of human activity is an attitude of "good enough" more deleterious than where horsemanship is concerned, for it is a form of sport requiring as much concentration and attention to detail and continuous effort as violin playing among the higher arts or golf among games. No one really learns to ride perfectly for there is always room for improvement; in its difficulty and variety lies its fascination, for those at least who are not content with superficial and sporadic results and prefer to dig at the root of things and their why's and wherefore's. It presents a never ending field of discoveries in ourselves and our mounts and a target of such magnitude that we are indeed obliged to aim at the mountains if we wish to hit even the modest hill top of presentable mediocrity.

As in the case of other arts, technique and continual work must be added to whatever natural inclination or talent we may possess if we really wish to emerge, and technique should be accepted in its most exacting form if we are to apply modern methods intelligently.

By constricting position and reactions within the bounds of perpendiculars and angles I have attempted to impress upon the reader the necessity for fully grasping the close mechanical relationship of various factors. If I underline to the point of pedantry certain principles which should be painstakingly and not casu-

PLATE 18

English steeplechase seat
Grand National

PLATE 19

The Times

English steeplechase
Grand National

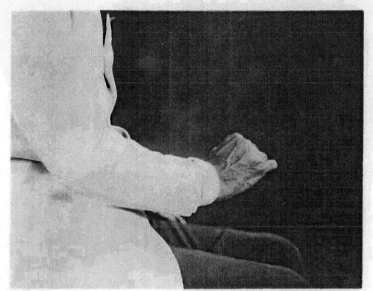

PLATE 20

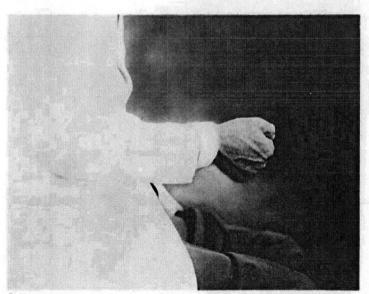

PLATE 21

ally interpreted, I am justified by the fact that no matter how conscientiously we shall strive to reach perfection it will at best ever remain all too evasive. How difficult it is to attain can be seen better by a careful study of photographs of even the most famous horsemen than by direct observation. Attitudes defective in some more or less essential detail, especially in the act of jumping, are met with among the best with discouraging frequency.

So far as the modern seat is concerned I cannot better conclude the advice I have tendered in the foregoing pages than by reiterating the importance of THE KNEE. No matter what — through our own fault, or the result of inevitable unforeseen emergencies — may be temporarily incorrect, the knee should never under any circumstances change its place; its joint acts as a hinge, but the knees themselves should remain as fixed to the saddle as if an iron bar had been run from one to the other through the body of the horse and riveted on each side.

The position of the foot, directly influenced by that of the ankle, has also been gone into, but while on the subject of possible and sometimes inevitable defects, particularly in jumping, we may say that if one were to choose between two evils, it is less serious to swing the foot back of the line C-D, as in Diagram A, than to thrust it forward towards the horse's shoulder (Plate

18). The former at least guarantees non-interference with the horse's head; the latter, on the contrary, is apt to result either in a violent jerk on the reins, through the body being thrown back, or in their being let slip through the fingers, resulting in loss of contact and control. Furthermore, it is easier and quicker to get back to a correct galloping attitude from the former position, even if — as is the case in Plate 25 — the knee has completely lost contact with the saddle flaps.

INSTINCT

Natural instincts are of little avail where horsemanship is concerned; in fact one of the first elements of good riding is what might be called the reversal of spontaneous impulses, and it is only when this inversion has sunk thoroughly into our sub-consciousness that we are eventually able to do the right thing. We all know, for example, that the more we pull on a horse's mouth the more he takes hold and that if we follow this instinct the only result is intense discomfort and a muck sweat for both of us. If we put a child, or even a grown person who has never before ridden, on the back of a horse he will probably do everything he should not: hold on by his heels by placing them as tightly as possible against the horse's side, toes down and knees away from the saddle, round his back and hang on to the reins for dear life. If the horse has not by this time bolted down the road and we dare, after a few moments of agonizing trotting and cantering, put our greenhorn over even the smallest of jumps, we will see him jerk his body back with his hands to his chin, the legs either wrapped still closer around the horse's barrel or thrust out straight before him in another typically "instinctive" attitude. All this has to be demolished and another mentality carefully built in its stead — the mentality that by reversal of impulse will bring horse and rider into accord. The latter, by his superior intelligence, must adapt his balance and poise to the horse, which is exactly what the Italian expression *equitazione naturale* is meant to convey — naturalness for the horse, not instinctively for the man.

In this connection it would not come amiss to go into the horse's balance as understood in the Italian method, but this would lead me far beyond the limits of this book, for it is not a subject that can be dealt with in a few words or even a few pages, without running the risk of misinterpretations and misconceptions. I shall limit myself therefore to refuting the idea frequently held by the uninitiated — and that I have even seen set down in black and white — to the effect that Italian horses are unbalanced and "all on the shoulder," by stating that this point, like that of the seat, needs careful study and a complete grasp of fundamental principles before it can be judged fairly.

[41]

SIMPLICITY

This is a word which should be ever present in our minds when considering the means human ingenuity has devised for exploiting the horse.

Having established the position which gives the best balance and poise to the man and concedes the greatest freedom of action, compatible with control, to the horse, and having adopted a saddle that most contributes to these desiderata, we should rely on our own reflective and studious ability, rather than on complicated accessories, for getting the best and most out of our mounts. Hence the elimination of all severe bits and a preference for the plain snaffle — aided at most by a running martingale, which, if of the proper length, is no martingale at all! Breast plate and martingale undoubtedly dress a horse and look well, a bare shoulder giving somehow the naked look we associate with the circus ring, but apart from the consideration that these subsidiaries contribute to smartness, their value is negligible. The only real martingale is the hand.

A lot of time, breath and ink are wasted in discussing the various merits of bridles, bits, nose bands and other contrivances for overcoming, rather than correcting, the defects of the horse — hours and reams of paper which would be better employed in studying the defects and shortcomings of the horseman. If man had always gone on the assumption that he has as much, if not more, to learn than the animal he bestrides, we would not have had to wait centuries for the discovery of principles as plain and conclusive as the egg of Columbus.

THE CRITIC

Should it appear that certain details I have dwelt on are too obvious to be worthy of particular mention and some of the things I have specially stressed are what all horsemen past the beginner's stage already know, I can only repeat what I have already said in the foregoing pages, namely, that if theoretically we are sometimes wise, in practice — mainly because it is difficult to see ourselves as others see us — we signally fail to apply what we preach. If we are to admit that well-known amateurs (civilians) who spend much time in the saddle for years on end are riders — I do not go so far as to say horsemen — worthy of the name and that their photographs, especially in the act of jumping, deserve the glowing captions which frequently accompany them, I must reiterate what I have already written in this respect: that these same photographs — of which I have a large and exhilarating collection under my eyes — are principally instructive in that they show us what should not be done — and their main value lies in the demonstration they give of how difficult it really is, after all, to fall off a horse!

[43]

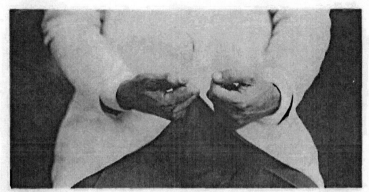

PLATE 22

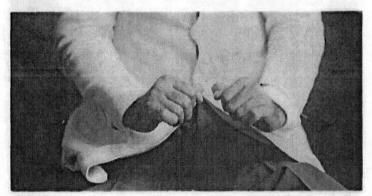

PLATE 23

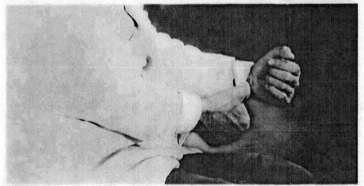

PLATE 24

PLATE 25   *Wide World Photos*

American steeplechase

PLATE 26

Good examples of contact, astride and sidesaddle

CHAPTER III

CONTACT VS. WINGS

CONTACT — the pressure on the horse's mouth
exercised by the rider's hands through the
reins for the control of pace and direction —
should be conceived as continuous and not intermittent.

It has been drummed into all horsemen and especially those of the younger generations that the horse in
jumping must have his head; apparently, however,
teachers sometimes fail to qualify this excellent advice
and pupils, in their anxiety to conform to instructions,
throw their body forward several yards before they
reach the jump — generally without properly rising
in the saddle — round their backs, point their toes to
the ground, and leaving the reins flapping in the
breeze, trust to their horses — and Providence — to
land them safely on the far side. This kind of approach
would be bad enough if performed as the horse rises
to the jump, but it is still worse when carried out —

as is the case nine times out of ten when the jump is provided with wings — the moment the horse's nose is inside the latter. When the wings are inordinately long, as happens in most schooling grounds and in some show rings, the result is that the horse is his own master for several strides.

Riders of this school — and they abound to an incredible degree — are at best incapable of obliging their mounts to face the obstacle where and how they — the riders — desire. The object of wings unfortunately being to keep the horse within bounds and thereby diminish the difficulty of the performer in the saddle, we may well ask ourselves why such difficulties should be thus diminished and to what purpose. The rider past the beginner's stage, — and no other should appear in show ring or hunting field — should not have to rely on such expedients and should always have his horse under sufficient control to oblige him to jump where he, and not the horse — chooses; this is obviously impossible if the reins are relinquished even one single stride before taking off. Wings are barely admissible in the riding school; their continued use, once the tyro phase is passed, can only result in grievous defects of position and style. They furthermore develop in the rider a completely false instinct as to when and to what degree to leave his horse alone; incidentally the latter phrase does not mean that contact

should ever be suppressed for in *no case* should reins
ever be slack, loose reins *not* being synonymous with
good hands. If we are told *ad nauseam* that the horse
must be free at his jumps, that he is not to be interfered with because he needs his head and neck to keep
his balance during the various phases of leaping, and
that he must therefore enjoy a certain amount of liberty, we are not very often enlightened as to the exact
moment in which to apply these principles nor told
that, until the right instant, the horse must be well
under control and not left to jump where and how he
pleases, or even not to jump at all! It may safely be
said that eighty per cent of the run-outs, refusals, and
"sloppy" performances in show ring and hunting field
are due to this inaccurate conception, and consequent
avoidance, of the rider's duties; the fault may be
largely laid at the door of most instructors' peculiar
weakness for wings, which may simplify their task
but renders an ill service to their pupils. If we are to
assume, as I think we always should when thinking
of, writing about or discussing anything connected
with horsemanship — that its only touchstone is to vis-
ualize it as a means of crossing a natural country, we
should strive to evolve the system most suited to enable
us, under changing conditions of pace and terrain, to
negotiate varied and unexpected obstacles with safety
and despatch. It therefore stands to reason that if we

[47]

get into the habit of relying on artificial help to get us over jumps we will ever be unprepared for the rougher and more close-to-nature form of riding — the only true basis of all equitation, the oldest, in fact the original, association between horse and man: the chace.

An acquaintance of mine successfully follows drags (frequently to their end through fairly stiff runs) without the slightest attempt on the part of his mount to jump anywhere but in the very centre of the numerous "panels" intersecting the line. He is the fortunate possessor of an intelligent and reliable old Irish hunter who seems to know which side his oats are buttered on and how important it is to preserve in our superiors the illusion of their high efficiency. His owner, with a determination worthy of a better cause, having adopted the position shown in Figure 1, would in no way be able to prevent a refusal or a run-out to either side of the panel where, on the particular lines I have in mind, there is generally no fence to jump at all!* The old horse seems to realize how difficult it is in these hard times to keep a comfortable job and a good home and therefore carries his unsophisticated master conscientiously over the exact places he should go if he were riding instead of merely being carried — thereby giv-

* This is a peculiarity of some American drags which have jumps built in the middle of a field

[48]

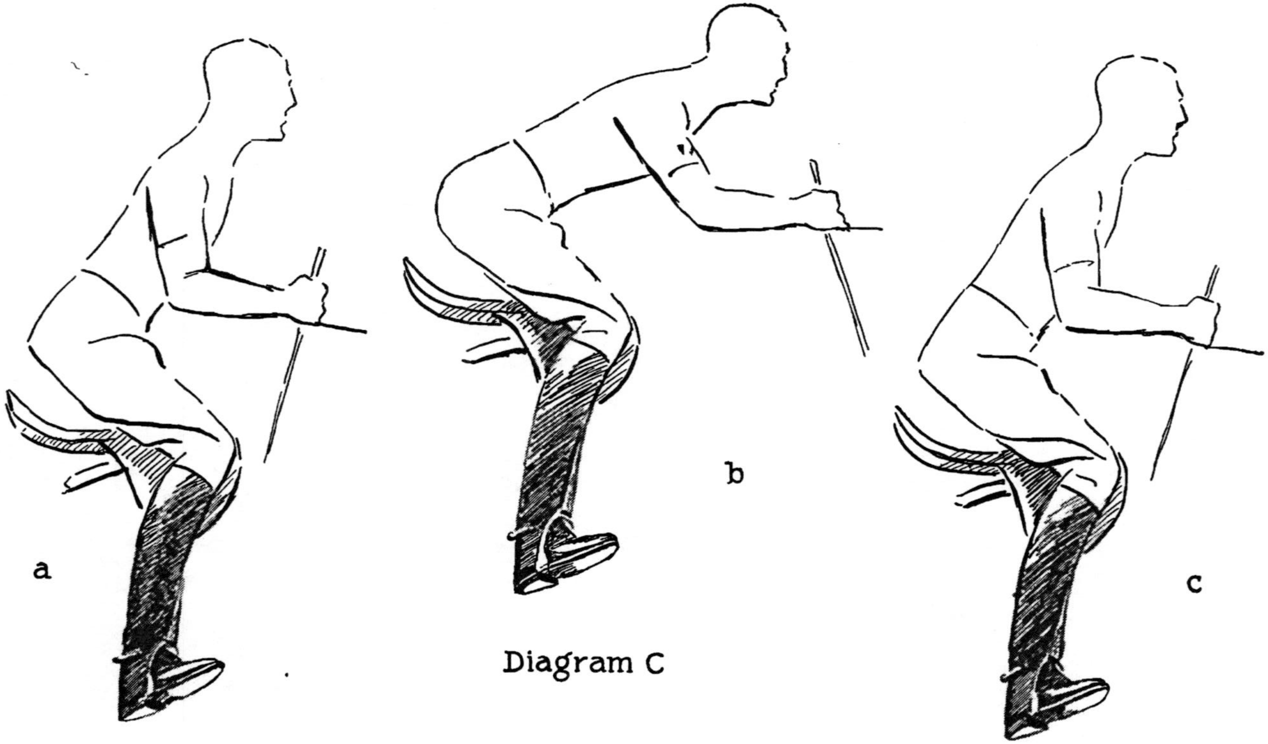
a
b
c

Diagram C

ing him a very good time and a huge opinion of himself. The "Irishman" is of course the pet of the stable but I cannot help wondering, as I look at his intelligent old face as he is led away to the van covered in warm blankets at the end of the day, whether he merely blinks his eyes — or winks!

Not all of us are fortunate enough to possess animals of such sense (or sense of humour), nor perhaps would we all want them, fool-proof conveyances possessing as a rule a consistent and conservative but somewhat plodding style of getting over a country which does not appeal to the more enterprising among us. But on the other hand, if we are ambitious enough to desire more sporting rides we should remember, among other things, that natural fences, or even American "panels" and "chicken coops," do not grow wings, and therefore suppress them in schooling grounds and horse shows as well.

Let us draw a comparison between Figure 1 (illustrating the position kept practically unaltered throughout approach, jump and landing by a certain category of horsemen, aided and abetted by the faithful wings) and Diagram C (a, b, c). I have advisedly placed "b" above "a" and "c" to represent correct position at the top of the jump, while the two latter are identical to demonstrate that the rider should regain the exact posture, on landing and galloping on, that he had on approaching and taking off. There are naturally intermediate positions of the body which only a slow motion film could possibly illustrate and the changes from "a" to "b" and from "b" to "c" should be understood to be gradual and in smooth synchronic rhythm with the action of the horse.

To return to the question of contact, it will easily be seen that if the positions "a," "b" and "c" are applied in place of that in Figure 1 the rider will be jumping with the horse and not merely being carried over as a dead — even if not actively interfering — weight. He will furthermore be in control through every phase without in any way meddling with his horse's head, which he will be "giving him," — without sacrificing contact, — by leaning, not throwing, the body forward, increasing the angle between thigh and calf and following the horse's mouth with his hands.

It is evident that with firm and equal pressure on each side of his mouth and with the rider's hands in correct position of control, legs in the right place and exercising the proper grip with knees and calves, it is easy:

First: To regulate the horse's pace before and immediately after the jump.

Second: To choose for him the exact spot where we wish him to face and surmount his fence.

FIGURE 4

Toe down, loose knee equals loose seat

FIGURE 5.

Toe down, legs back: The least incorrect of the incorrect positions

Third: To discourage successfully any possible attempt at refusals or untidy and crooked jumping.

The camera being often more convincing than words
and sketches I refer the reader to Plate 26 which shows
contact, and thereby control and direction at a glance.
The figure on the horse jumping being that of a lady
is of peculiar interest, for she is in position "b" of
Diagram B as applied to side saddle, while the officer,
whose horse is just galloping on after jumping, is a
perfect photographic version of "a" or "c" if we wish
to imagine him on the opposite side of the wall in any
of the strides immediately preceding the take-off.

PLATE 27
Forward position with comparatively long leathers

PLATE 28
Use of whip without change of position

CHAPTER IV

AIDS AND JUMPING

THE sharp-rowelled spur has practically disappeared from civilized use, which should be a subject of congratulation even independently of humanitarian considerations. Among other drawbacks it caused a horse to shorten his stride and therefore defeated its end as a means of increasing pace; and as with modern methods the infliction of severe punishment is extremely rare, the blunt spur is all that is needed in any but the most extraordinary circumstances, the proper use of the leg being an excellent substitute.

Although the general impression abroad apparently is that Italians are prevented by their shorter leathers from using their legs to any extent, if there is actually a school in the world in which the lower limbs have their full share it is precisely the Italian which, as has

[57]

already been said, is not *based* on the short leather
(Plate 27). Like everything else connected with this
method, the use of the leg is so subtle as to escape the
eye of the uninitiated. It consists of well regulated
pressure of knee and calf, with the least possible movement of the foot; devotees of the "kicking" method
and of a free and enthusiastic use of the heel are therefore naturally led to believe that the Italian use of the
leg is so limited as to be almost negligible. On the contrary, taught as the Italians are to jump even the nar-
rowest obstacles without wings, their legs play as important a part in keeping the horse straight and at the
desired pace as the hands, and they are further very
effective means of more or less gentle coercion.

The use of both whip and spur is two-fold: aid and
punishment. They are employed as aids to encourage
a horse or signal our wishes to him, or as punishment,
to communicate our displeasure and impose our will
on him as against his own. In the first case their use
should be mild, in the second severe and determined—
but sparing.

There are few more difficult things than their proper
application. Punishment especially should be resorted
to in a manner so discriminating and so just that no
doubt should remain in the horse's mind as to its exact
purport, otherwise misunderstanding and confusion
are the result. Excessive chastisement is always to be

avoided, rough-riding methods having nowadays been relegated to the prairies and the steppes. One sharp cut with the whip applied at the right time is better than a prolonged thrashing, no matter how grave the misdemeanour.

The whip as a signal is really so difficult to apply that it is only given to such as know the finer points of the game to use it to advantage, at the right time and with the right tempo. Nothing more clearly differentiates, even to the spectator's eye, the amateur from the professional than its use in the finish of a race, and if its cadence is of the greatest importance on the flat it is even more so in jumping. A cut too soon may so puzzle a horse as to throw him out of stride with disastrous results; a blow applied too close to a fence may turn a sensible refusal or a clever "buck" jump into the most appalling of "purlers." The best advice therefore that one can tender the average horseman is to tread very gingerly on this particular ground and never be tempted to solve sudden dilemmas with the whip; patient and gentle but determined schooling in the paddock should eliminate the necessity of either whip aid or whip punishment in the field. The latter is in any case eliminated when riding to hounds by the fact that a crop is carried, with which any but the most brutal chastisement is impossible.

[59]

As the whip should always be applied on the quarters it should be used with the free hand — right or left as may be required — by momentarily putting the reins in the other (Plate 28). "Tapping" on the shoulder by twitching the wrist of a hand already engaged with the rein or reins results in an involuntary action of that side on the horse's mouth which only disturbs and confuses him, for the whip urges while the rein deters.

It is in our day a truism to say that the pace at which we should approach a jump depends on its size (height and/or width), the going and take-off, the inclination of the ground and the quality of the terrain; the merest tyro should know this at least theoretically. What really matter more are the abstract principles for approaching and surmounting a jump, and although it is impossible to tender advice so varied as to fit the infinite assortment of emergencies that may arise, particularly in the hunting field, rules of general application can to a certain extent be established.

Position having already been dealt with, it remains for us — where jumping is concerned — to consider how we can best assist the horse. That he is to be left "free at his jumps" would be insufficiently qualified advice, for "assisting"* should not be limited to non-

* The Italian word is *assecondare*, the exact meaning of which is untranslatable. The nearest English approach would be "help without interference."

interference but extended rather to bringing him to the obstacle and seeing him over it in those conditions of balance best calculated to land us both safely on the far side.

We all know that, whenever possible, jumps should be faced at right angles to the direction of approach; also that a horse should be steadied some distance away, especially if the jump is a stiff one (timber or wall) at which the horse should be as collected as circumstances and the time at our disposal permit.

For us to be in full control as we approach the obstacle we should have our reins (two or four as the case may be) separate; the right in our right hand and the left in our left. Pace we regulate by a harmonious blending of contact and leg pressure and by their variations suppress any tendency to swerve, hesitate or refuse. A continuous vibration of the leg from the knee down will prove effective — this "pulsating" action to be initiated the moment we sense any intention on the part of the horse to do anything but face his obstacle determinedly; it should be increased, diminished or stopped according to his reaction to it. The moment we have decided in our mind the exact spot where we intend to jump we should *gradually* steady our mount as we approach it. The horse will thus jump in his stride without loss of either time or impetus, important factors in hunting to say nothing of racing. In the show ring and particularly in those jumping classes where time is no object, we can afford to go slower and fit our pace more carefully to the size and quality of the jump, but in the field "measuring" should be to a great degree sacrificed to the necessity for galloping on.

Only when we have to deal with an over-keen horse with an inclination to rush his fences should we take one or more strong pulls half a dozen strides from the jump so as to bring his hocks under him too near the obstacle to allow of his again getting out of hand before he reaches it; but this should also be accomplished without any jerky or rough action on the horse's mouth and preferably with a particularly strong version of the screw-like turn of the wrist previously described.

How and to what extent may we venture to assist the horse in jumping?

As a horse takes his final measurement of the size of his jump, in the stride in which he takes off, by thrusting his head forward and down (Diagram D, "2"), the rider should promptly respond to this mechanical request for greater freedom. This should be done, not by allowing the reins to slide through the fingers, but by following with the hands, or the wrists, or both, the gradually increasing extension of the horse's head and neck. For us suddenly to relinquish contact altogether in the jumping stride or worse still,

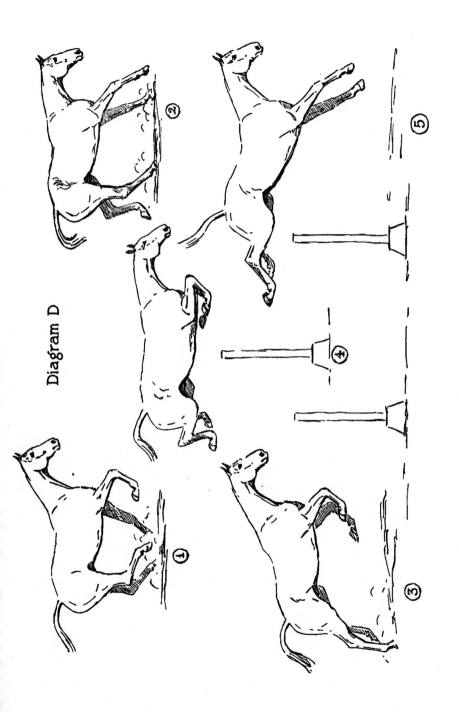

Diagram D

sooner (Figure 1) — thereby unbalancing him — is as great a mistake as preventing him from taking accurate stock of the obstacle by forcibly holding his head up.

The *second* movement the horse accomplishes is to bring his head up again as he gets back on his quarters prior to the actual take-off, in which phase the rider's hands return towards the body, momentarily increasing contact ever so slightly during that fraction of a second before the horse, having propelled himself off the ground, ("3") again stretches out his neck ("4") — this time to the utmost — in the effort of throwing the weight of his "balancier" over the jump. This *third* movement should be accompanied by the rider not only with the hands and the wrists, (Plate 26), but by leaning forward from the loins as well, while increasing the angle between calf and thigh (Diagram C, "b") and preserving *lightened contact on the same length of rein*. As the horse's head gradually returns to position ("1") of Diagram D, when his quarters begin their descent towards the ground, the rider's hands are again drawn more towards the body which gradually assumes a less inclined position, the angle between calf and thigh being correspondingly diminished and contact increased (fourth movement).

The landing phase of the jump is as important as

[65]

the take-off. Using the ankle and, to a lesser degree, the knee joint as shock absorbers, the rider should without brusque or sudden movements very evenly begin to slip back — loins bent inwards — to the galloping position (end of fourth movement) as the horse's hind feet touch the ground. Bumping back into the saddle is not only tiring to the horse and on the long run becomes even so painful as to disgust him with jumping altogether, but may cause him to drop his quarters too soon and hit or knock down upright obstacles and not completely clear wide ones such as ditches or brooks, thus contributing, in the show ring to an undesirable accumulation of penalties, and in the hunting field to possible falls.

It cannot be sufficiently stressed that smoothness of execution in every detail is the *sine qua non* of good horsemanship; jumping in particular, in itself a violent effort, should be rendered as easy and as pleasant as possible for both horse and man by every means in our power.

The slow-motion camera is invaluable for the study of the above described phases but the only way practically to "sense" them and to develop to the point of instinct our ability to conform to them, is systematically to jump our horse slowly over fair-sized rails or walls; the consecutive movements, notably the thrust forward of the head of the first stage of the jump become less noticeable the faster we go, because the time taken by each phase diminishes in direct ratio to the pace we are travelling. When, on the contrary, a horse is obliged to take his time over obstacles of any importance, the various movements, being more laborious, are more distinct, the horse supplementing what he lacks in impetus by greater and slower muscular effort. Some horses accentuate the movements of head and neck more than others.

At no time before, during or after the jump should we lean our hands on the withers or neck, or sides of either; any fixed position of the hands prevents our following the movements of the horse's head with them and as the reins should never be allowed to slip through the fingers, deliberately keeping the fists in one place can only result in interference with the horse's action, —unless we place them so far towards the horse's ears that contact is completely ignored and the proper position of the body, and therefore its balance, destroyed. If the body is correctly poised there will be no jar in any phase of the jump and no necessity for steadying *points d'appui* other than the knees and stirrups.

Italian saddle without knee rolls

Italian saddle with knee rolls

English saddle

CHAPTER V

SADDLES

I HAVE assumed in the preceding pages that anyone wishing to cultivate the forward seat has
begun by discarding the old-fashioned straight
type of saddle, which is not adapted to modern methods principally because, if the leathers are the right
length,* the knees are perforce pushed forward beyond the limits of the straight flaps. This is so inevitable that it happens even when an approximate form
of forward seat is adopted such as shown in Figure 2,
for, as soon as thigh and tibia reach anything approaching the proper angle in relation to each other,
additional curve in the flaps becomes indispensable.
Furthermore, the Italian saddle—of which many more
or less accurate imitations are now made in England
and Germany — is placed much further up the withers

* The Italians never use the expression "short" leather, but say "right
length of leather" *(staffatura giusta).*

and nearer the shoulder and its entire shape is different (Plate 31). The tree is wider and the actual seat
more concave, the padding under it thicker — the latter point being of particular importance as the saddle
should never tip back. The whole saddle is softer and
more supple and by use moulds itself to the rider's
shape much more than the harder and flatter English
type.

The Italian saddle is in a sense more difficult to fit
properly for the very reason that it must *fit* and cannot merely be slapped on; it should be adapted with
painstaking care and in cases of peculiar conformation, such as very high and narrow withers or a sway
back, requires special adaptation and the permanent
use of one individual saddle fitted once for all to a
particular animal.

The centre of gravity of the old-fashioned type cor-
responds to the vertical of the stirrup leathers, which
when hanging loose, practically divide the flaps in two
equal parts (Plate 32), in the Italian variety, on the
contrary, the leathers when hanging straight have behind them only a small proportion of the flaps, a good
two-thirds of which remain in front of them (Plate
31), but, contrary to what might be supposed, the properly adjusted Italian saddle keeps its place much more
securely and snugly than the old-fashioned straight one
and never calls for the complicated "Dutch collars"

which nowadays all too frequently offend the eye on steeplechase and point-to-point courses. The conformation of some horses is supposed to exact these extraordinary appliances, but I am inclined to think that in most cases it is the shape of the saddle which is to blame — to say nothing of the rider's shifting weight, due to loose knees. The padding under the flaps of the Italian saddle being practically all in front of the girths, the pressure of the latter pushes it forward towards the shoulder and the "perched" poise of the forward seat itself contributes to concentrating the pressure in the right place, i.e., towards the withers.

Knee rolls form an integral part of this saddle. I have heard them described as "unsporting;" in my opinion one might just as well describe any other part of the saddle as drastically. Rolls are artificial aids, but so are stirrups and seat and the flaps themselves of whatever variety. If we were to follow this line of reasoning to its logical end we would have to conclude that the only "sporting" way of riding is bareback. Knee rolls, we admit, do not improve the appearance of a saddle, but this aesthetic defect can be overcome by substituting for them a correspondingly thicker padding in the under part of the saddle where the knee rests. This provides the necessary purchase and leaves the saddle itself purer in line (Plate 30).

As to the exact degree of influence that the Italian

saddle has on the "perched" seat, obviously a saddle
with flaps curved forward contributes to the comfort
and even safety of the rider, but we must not thereby
conclude that the forward or "perched" position *as
such* is entirely dependent on it. I have travelled
much and not always had my own gear with me with
which to enjoy a ride or even an occasional day to
hounds, and yet, when confronted with even the
straightest and hardest specimens of the English
variety, I have never found it necessary to alter
the position I would have kept on my own saddle.
My knees, to be sure, sometimes protruded well
beyond the flaps and rested on thin air, but I man-
aged with a minimum of discomfort not to relapse
into the position of my early youth,* by an exaggeration of the ankle twist already fully dwelt on.
It was under these conditions that some years ago
I rode to hounds in England in a very fast run of
eighty minutes without a check — and the fact that,
though I had not been on the back of a horse for six
months, I finished well up over a stiff country, in
heavy going and on a hireling I had never even seen
before, speaks, I think, not badly for the Italian seat
as a hunting seat. Incidentally, I am convinced that I
owe not losing the latter half of the run to the fact that
my horse, having dropped his quarters in a ditch on the

* See Preface.

[72]

far side of a fence, was able to scramble out promptly and continue, thanks to my being well forward in the saddle on landing. The hunt, so far as I was concerned, would have had a different ending had I been *sitting* my saddle.

Felt numnahs are in such general use in some countries, Italy among them, that saddles are not considered complete without them; though some people object to the looks of them they indisputably contribute to the comfort of both horse and rider and, by acting as a soft buffer between two harder surfaces — horse and saddle — eliminate all possibility of sore backs and help mould the saddle comfortably to the horse, an important point, especially in hilly countries.

PLATE 33

Toe down; knee out of place

PLATE 34

Increased thigh and tibia angle

CHAPTER VI

BRIDLES AND MARTINGALES

I KNOW of one case of a family hunting all their horses in excessively long-cheeked bits and standing martingales. I regret never having had occasion to ask on what principle such a system can possibly be applied to a sport which requires the maximum of freedom for the horse's head,* for it would have been interesting to know why *all* the inmates of any one stable should have to have their powers constricted by such severe steel and leather combinations.

I might give, as outstanding examples at the other end of the scale, people who school their horses to the complications of the *haute école* in plain broken snaffles, and those rare polo players who use nothing more severe than snaffles and running martingales.

Any tune required can be played on a horse's mouth

* "The horse should cross a country with the freedom of a hound"
Colonel R Ubertalli.

with a snaffle, for all depends on the capability of the performer; the greater it happens to be the more simple the instrument needed — the more limited it is, the more help he will require from the power given by leverage. There are, of course, horses whose mouths are past redemption; in these cases the severer the bit the lighter the hand required, but as a general rule a horseman's ability, so far as his hands are concerned, can almost be measured — in inverse ratio — from the weight of the steel in his horse's mouth.

Between the two extremes quoted above, runs the whole gamut of that moot question — bitting — one of the most inexhaustible subjects of discussion among horsemen the world over, but which in reality can be reduced to remarkably few principles.

It can reasonably be asserted that if it were possible for a horseman always to use horses broken and schooled by himself the plain snaffle would reign supreme, as indeed it does in some countries, Italy among them. Bad mouths are made, not born, but as horses generally come to us after having been through a greater or lesser variety of adventures, hardness of mouth and similar acquired defects are often past correction and therefore oblige us to have recourse to the more complicated varieties of mouth gear. Even defects of conformation, such as ewe-necks or badly put on heads are not sufficient reason for using anything but snaffles, provided it is possible with time and knowledge to "remake" a horse by patient schooling.

It is not given to all to possess superlative hands and ability and we cannot blame the lesser lights among us for using whatever gear gives the best results — and that promptly — for their particular purposes; it is nevertheless undeniable that a horseman worthy of the name should not need more than three varieties of bridles in his stable: the snaffle, the Weymouth (plain double) and the Pelham. Only very exceptional cases justify the use of jaw-breaking types of bits, gags, standing martingales and other instruments of torture. No horse that has not been pulled about roughly in his early years should ever prove unridable in a plain snaffle — even when in high hunting condition; if he does, the cause of the trouble should be looked for not in his mouth but much farther up — at the other end of the reins.

It is always difficult to generalize; no two horses are alike and no two horsemen, even among horses and horsemen of the highest possible type. Since the greatest distinguishing differences lie precisely in the mouths of the former and the hands of the latter we may conclude that in each separate case they will have mutually to find the bitting of peace and understanding — but always within the limits of a scale running at most from the plain snaffle — which is practically

[77]

the only bit used by Italian cavalry officers — to an ordinary double bridle, via the various Pelhams.

Concerning the latter: no bit has been so widely discussed and none has had so much said or written about it, pro and con, as the Pelham; in the cloud of verbiage that has always surrounded it, its particular uses or usefulness have not yet been made clear.

The Pelham after all is nothing but a combination of bit and snaffle on the same mouthpiece, and is supposed to be lighter than the former and stronger than the latter. One theory concerning it is that it should be used as a whole, that is to say always with pressure equal on the four reins, radically differing in this respect from the real double bridle on which of course the play of the fingers on each separate rein allows of infinitesimal shadings of touch and contact. This simplification has never been my personal conception of the use of the Pelham, for I am inclined to think that if it has any advantages at all — which some deny — they consist in the fact that if we employ the upper or snaffle reins, leaving the bit reins loose or looser, its action on the bars is precisely that of the snaffle — whereas if necessary we can bring into play the lower or bit reins which, by leverage on the cheek-bars and curb chain, act, in a milder form, like the bit of the double bridle. The mouthpiece of the Pelham, being thicker than the bridoon of the double bridle, is less severe and

[78]

therefore practically no harsher than the ordinary snaffle, if used independently of the bit. If on the other hand we are to eliminate the use of the separate reins it is difficult to see what admissible purpose it answers.

The broken Pelham is, in a sense, the most fool-proof of bits, and as such it is ideal for getting children used to four reins without too much disturbing the horse's mouth and at the same time giving the necessary control that a plain snaffle cannot exercise in the hands of a novice or the very young. For similar reasons and also because soldiers even of the mounted arms cannot all have good hands — recruited as they are mostly from the peasant class — the Pelham is now the regulation bit of the Italian army,* as it was found to constitute the happy medium between the snaffle and the double bridle and a great improvement on the very severe double Hanoverian in use in the old days.

A new type of Pelham has appeared in the show ring within the last two years, evidently based on the above mentioned theory that both reins are to be used with equal pressure. This new device consists in a single-rein Pelham, the upper and lower rings of the cheek-piece being joined together close to the horse's mouth by a loop to which the rein is attached. We had

* When on duty officers are obliged to relinquish the snaffle that by preference they use on every other occasion

before seen something very similar in the shape of what can only be described as a double-single bridle or Pelham — the two reins on either side coming together a few inches from the hand — a device which already eliminated all possibility of independent play of upper or lower reins — but the last version is so further simplified as to represent a still franker confession on the rider's part of his incapacity of handling with the necessary artistry either a plain snaffle or a double bridle — rather like having resort to playing the piano with one's fists instead of one's fingers! This contrivance may, and probably does, answer certain show ring purposes, such as enabling the rider to hold a pulling jumper around the ring with little or no hand technique — a short cut to efficiency which is no more to be included in the "art" of horsemanship than coloured photographs can be substituted for paintings.

The martingale plays no essential part in the Italian method and I only deal with it because horsemen of other schools might fail to understand my completely ignoring it.

The only martingale admissible and not in contradiction with the principles we have dealt with is the running variety applied to the snaffle or bridoon reins at its proper length, i.e., measured by raising the rings to the horse's withers. Thus adjusted, it does more to keep the horse's head in place by its weight — which is slight — and straight by side pressure — which is slighter still — than, as is generally and unreflectingly supposed, to keep it down. To make any appreciable impression in the vertical sense it has to be so short as to constitute an impediment irritating to both horse and man. If, in exceptional cases, the use of comparatively strong bits may be condoned, the same latitude cannot be extended to very short running martingales and still less to the standing varieties.

CHAPTER VII

CONTROVERSY

ALTHOUGH the object of this book is not to make invidious comparisons between the old and the new, the "back" and the "forward" position, the "long" and the "short" leather, but rather to attempt to convey a clear conception of what the forward seat really consists in, I cannot refrain from expressing the surprise common to all my countrymen that it should still, in Anglo-Saxon countries, be qualified as "controversial"— after thirty years of vigorous life and all invading vitality.

In this connection I am tempted for one brief moment to enter the polemical field and quote one of the highest authorities on the Italian seat living, who, in my opinion, has with the following words, "cut the Gordian knot" of all discussions pro and con the position his master, Captain Caprilli, evolved and taught:

"When it will have been proved that a horseman

sliding freely in the saddle disturbs the horse less than an immovable one; that by *not following the horse's neck* in its every movement — including the descending phase of the jump — we help the horse instead of interfering with him; that by *resting thighs and buttocks* on his ribs and his spinal column we increase, instead of diminish, his powers, and finally that the horseman is safer and more comfortable *without a secure point d'appui on the stirrups* — only then will we be ready to admit that the votaries of the long leather* are right."† The italics are mine.

The contribution of the forward seat to the comfort and security of both man and horse is not yet generally appreciated; if this position is still looked at askance in some quarters, we must lay the blame at the door of its illegitimate versions which, when condemned, get nothing more than they deserve.

---

* i e , old system (Author's note)

† Colonel R. Ubertalli. *La Staffatura* Il Cavallo Italiano. February, 1925.

PLATE 35
"Standing" position. Leg too straight, knee out of place

PLATE 36
*Crouched or "kneeling" position—result of toe down and
rounded back*

CHAPTER VIII

Blue, Red and Yellow

I HOPE I have made it sufficiently clear in the preceding pages that the forward seat should not be considered only as a show ring jumping seat; it is part and parcel of cross-country riding (Equitazione di Campagna) and originally created with this object in view. The ring and its jumping competitions, as we now know them, were an afterthought.

I have been obliged to illustrate this book principally with photographs taken at horse shows — and as a hunting man with little use for arc lights and bands I feel almost like apologizing to such of my readers as may be like-minded. It is only in this way, however, that I was enabled to illustrate the points I have discussed. Just as it is impossible to observe one's neighbour profitably in the hunting field, no photographs of actual cross-country riding — especially to hounds — are procurable and we are therefore obliged to fall back on the infinitely instructive variety of the numberless pictures taken at the ring-side; being mostly of jumps, they are particularly useful and to the point for didactic purposes in this particular connection, as they permit the underlining of virtues and defects by comparison and juxtaposition. We can at least be grateful to the show ring for this, although horse shows as such — like most institutions of their kind — defeat their own ends.

As dog show canines are often so highly bred that they are deaf or stupid or both, the horse show animal is all too frequently no earthly use outside the ring. Hunting people know how rash it is to buy a hunter from the tanbark and how a bona fide hunter is rarely a good or willing performer in the ring. Crossing a natural country and going more or less faultlessly over a series of enclosed jumps, even if often very much bigger — but always better placed — than are likely to be met with when following hounds,— are two very different propositions — and as I have already stated when writing about riding and jumping, I must assume that we should always have in mind pure and legitimate sport and not games. Horse shows, with rare exceptions,* contribute nothing to the improve-

* For example, those which make a specialty of breeding classes

ment of breeding and very little to that of horsemanship.

Even setting aside certain classes of horses such as
"park hacks" and Kentucky saddle horses, on which I
am in no way qualified to pass judgment but which are
all too evidently purely artificial products whose utility
may well be questioned, such specimens of horse flesh
as appear under the present day ring conceptions and
rules as "hunters" hardly respond to the requirements
that such a description implies. The "jumpers" have
at least the merit of not sailing under false colours, for
"jumpers" they are and absolutely nothing else.

We all have a right to our own points of view and to
amuse ourselves as we choose, but our particular hob-
bies should never, I think, be followed to the point of
distortion of fundamentals.

Horse show riding is a game which has strayed far
indeed from nature and natural conditions; let us
therefore not create confusion in our minds between
it and sport as conceived in the simpler days of Nimrod and Squire Osbaldeston.

The centuries-old association between man and
horse had its origin in the chace; the more we keep this
basic idea in mind the purer our diversions will be;
the farther we wander from it the more artificial will
they grow. In this mechanical age we should cling
more than ever — for the good of our bodies and souls

— to the few simple things that are left us and not allow arc lights, grand stands and applause to encroach on or get confused in our minds with the sky, green and brown fields, hedge and ditch and timber and the often unshared and purely personal and intimate satisfaction of finding one's way over a difficult country — far from white ties and hand clappings. There is contradiction in the very terms "sportsman" and "showman."

If the ribbons and flower pots of Olympia and Madison Square offend, we in Italy are by no means blameless. At the risk of making myself unpopular with such of my countrymen as may read these lines I must admit that although our "Concorsi Ippici" are always in the open air and the courses infinitely more difficult than any in the world — none excepted — they are in a sense the acme of uselessness from the practical point of view. In the first place, as they consist only of jumping classes over truly formidable obstacles none but the very highest class of specialized horseman stands the ghost of a chance; the result is that they are practically confined to *officers of the mounted arms in active service* and only to such as have made show jumping the study and hobby of their lives.* Apart

* The "Società Romana Equitazione," founded about two years ago, for the development and encouragement of amateur horsemanship, and now presided over by H. E. Achille Starace, Secretary of the Fascist Party, now holds in Rome frequent jumping competitions more adapted to the average rider than the official "Concorsi Ippici." Similar clubs, notably in Turin and Parma, are following this excellent example

[88]

from a few women who appear in ladies' classes, the civilians who dare attempt such competitions can be counted on the fingers of one hand and it is rare indeed for any of them to compare favourably with their military rivals even if, as is frequently the case, they are better mounted. This is only natural: few civilians, if any, have the opportunity for the first-class instruction and other facilities that the Army has to offer; furthermore the officer, and particularly the specialist, does practically nothing but ride with his own particular purpose in view. The show ring officer is a distinct type and rarely hunts or rides races, not because he would be incapable of doing so were he so minded, — as the sit-well-back brigade might suppose — but because he has developed that passion for ring competition which absorbs all his time and resources. On the other hand the hunting or racing officers seldom appear at the numberless "concorsi" that take place from Spring to Autumn from one end of the peninsula to the other. Some of us would prefer to see more uniforms at hunts, point-to-points and steeplechases and fewer in the arena, but unfortunately the ring seems to have an irresistible attraction for those who would undoubtedly be superlatively good in the more legitimate branches of the same art, for the exhibitions of high technique they give in the ring are truly marvelous.

[89]

What practical good are horse shows? I must begin
by admitting that our own in Italy are the most incomplete. At Olympia, in America and at Dublin and even
in Paris a certain variety of categories goes to make at
least a semblance of reasoned selection under different
heads; in many of them performance alone does not
count and the fact that hunters are also required to
meet certain standards of conformation, quality and
style of going, does to a certain extent contribute to
bringing out animals fitted perhaps for a little more
than getting over jumps without knocking them over,
but the utility of the ultimate results is nevertheless
not very convincing.

If the public knew sometimes what goes on behind
the scenes and what crocks and "bad actors" in private
do brilliantly in public, their unreasoning admiration
for the sleek animals that go back to their boxes adorn-
ed with all the colours of the rainbow would receive a
rude shock. Fortunately for their illusions, not one in
a hundred knows or really cares what it is all about and
are content with the thrill of seeing well-turned-out
horses more or less ably ridden, jumping one after
the other between monumental and well whitewashed
wings.

The nearest real test of a hunter other than the
hunting field are "hunter trials;" a horse that does
well in these competitions, as carried out in England

and America over natural courses and judged from a true hunting point of view can safely be termed a hunter and bought as such, if sound. No other competition is of the slightest use for forming an opinion on a cross-country conveyance; for it is unnecessary to add that animals farcically described as "hunters" under the present system of "qualifying" unfortunately enforced the world over and entered as such in certain point-to-points, are even more to be avoided by the hunting man than the show specimens, — for though they may have speed and blood they possess, as a rule, none of the qualities for a safe and comfortable ride to hounds.

Under existing conditions what do horse shows contribute to the improvement of riders or horses? The tanbark "hunters" are not hunters; the riders are either specialists in a class by themselves or all too amateurish amateurs; the good performers among the horses are useless for practical purposes for the reasons already stated, and from the breeding point of view as well, for, unlike the racing thoroughbred most of them are geldings — and even the mares are generally kept at the earning of ribbons and stakes till their time of usefulness for the stud is long past.

Horse shows are supposed to be a means of propaganda for hunting because many people first get interested in horse flesh through them and eventually graduate from the tanbark to the hunting field and even to the race course. To test the value of this assertion we would have to make a sort of census of how many real followers of hounds have begun their careers over the movable fences and carefully raked courses of country or town show rings; this being obviously impossible, I beg leave to doubt this statement which has never to my knowledge been backed by any convincing data. Personally I have generally found that the hunting and showing mentality and attitude of mind are fundamentally different and that there is little contact or sympathy between the two.

Show rings nevertheless are, or rather could be, of use observed from the proper angle, but in one respect only — the very one most obviously neglected by the hundreds and thousands of spectators who attend them, — namely, as a study of horsemanship for the collecting of "wrinkles" and the acquisition, through observation, of the finer points of riding — particularly jumping — and the avoidance of the more obvious mistakes and defects of style and technique. I have often been struck by the lack of critical sense of a horse show crowd; I have heard wild and most unmerited applause ignorantly lavished on the most extraordinarily bad performances and almost complete silence greet quieter but infinitely better riding. Thrashing and spurring a horse around the ring and knocking

everything over seems to be considered by these unsophisticated beings as the acme of pluck, dash, courage and ability, a smooth and less spectacular performance as tame and hardly worth the most languid
of hand claps — but if these same people gave themselves the trouble to observe the why's and wherefore's
of the difference between the two systems they might
perhaps learn something worth learning.

Comparisons are odious but may an Italian be allowed to say that striking exceptions to this collective
ignorance are the horse show crowds of his own country? Foreigners often remark with surprise the technical knowledge and intelligent appreciation displayed
by even the *hoi polloi* of Rome, Naples, Florence or
San Remo — and particularly the religious silence observed by tens of thousands of all classes of society
when watching with breathless interest the performance of horses and horsemen. Their thorough knowledge of the business in hand can only be compared to
that of an English crowd at a big cricket match, or
more aptly, to the Spanish *aficionados* of the bull ring
— whom they resemble in their tense excitement and
in their exuberant expression of approval.

Applause develops self-consciousness in the performer, especially if young. Note, for example the
smug air of self-satisfaction of the winner of a children's riding class.

[93]

In jumping events, which particularly lend themselves to dramatization, the acrobatics which thrill the ignorant are totally unnecessary and are the result of the histrionic spirit we all possess to a greater or lesser degree and which the presence of spectators encourages. The rider who consciously or unconsciously is posing for his or her friends will assume attitudes over 3 ft. 6 in. of brush that would be superfluous and out of place even over 5 ft. 6 in. of solid timber. This spirit is unfortunately the breath that keeps the show ring flame alive. Apart from professionals, how many of us would go from one show ring to another year after year if there was no one to look on?

The only real use of horse shows lies in *the improvement of horsemanship by observation and fastidious criticism* and this is the attitude of mind which should be encouraged in the public or at least such portions of it as are themselves actively interested in riding as a sport. This class of spectator should frequent the show ring in much the same spirit that a painter looks at a picture gallery or a musician listens to other musicians — for the improvement of his own art by absorption, study and criticism of fellow craftsmen's methods. If, on the contrary, we are to be content with superficial impressions and unsophisticated thrills we will follow horse shows with little profit. "Look more at the horseman than at the horse" should be our motto.

[94]

PLATE 37
A meet of the Roman fox-hounds on the Via Appia

PLATE 38
Correct position. Heavy weight

CHAPTER IX

The Chace

Like James I, in his *A King's Christian Dutie towards God,* "I cannot omit heere the hunting, namely, with running houndes, which is the most honourable and noblest sport thereof," to which, add I, the forward seat, properly understood and freed of the exaggerations and mannerisms the show ring has developed, is supremely adapted.

The only bona fide sport in the true sense of the word in which man and horse associate is cross-country riding in one form or another; of them all hunting takes precedence and when I say hunting I mean following the wild quarry, be it fox, stag, hare or boar. The carted stag is the best substitute, and drags, or even paper chases, if over a natural country, come next, though the unexpectedness of following the always unforeseen line of a live, and preferably wild, animal, is a much higher test of both horse and rider.

It is difficult to understand how it is possible even to discuss which is the more *complete* horseman — the cross-country rider or the show ring addict. The latter to be sure should possess very highly specialized technique, but the fact remains that he always knows his score, so to speak, beforehand, or has read so many similar scores that he has only to repeat himself *ad infinitum*. This applies particularly to America, where, apart from international courses, and such shows as Bryn Mawr, Devon and a few others, the only appreciable difference among them is the size of the ring.

The hunting man, on the other hand — always provided he intends to live with hounds — is every moment confronted with new problems requiring courage, coolness, intelligence, decision and judgment in the highest degree. Since we, like that much quoted sportsman Mr. Jorrocks, cannot disassociate in our minds sport from war, we require the former to bring out the qualities we would ask of a soldier. War and the chace have gone hand in hand through the centuries and are still the expression of deeply rooted instincts of a primitiveness which should not be deformed by love of the purely spectacular or emasculated by artificialities.

Hunting is supposed to be a rich man's pursuit and it is indeed apt to run into money if we want the best of everything and plenty of it. In certain communities, overblessed with this world's goods, this is the prevailing attitude to such a degree that the more unassuming members do not dare appear at the covert-side if not mounted at least as well as the Joneses, but the man with the long purse will never know how much more real satisfaction can be got out of a limited stable, or even one horse, chosen and bought with judgment and care, than out of a dozen animals purchased perhaps by wire from a photograph, a pedigree or on the recommendation of a dealer. The pleasure of turning an apparent "dud," taken perhaps out of ignorant or incapable hands, with painstaking attention into a useful and sometimes brilliant hunter, will ever remain a closed book to him, for such horses represent one's own handiwork and knowledge, not merely the tangible expression of a generous bank account.

In many quarters there is a decided tendency to run to quantity — very often, to be sure, joined with quality — but entirely out of proportion to the work in hand. In these conditions it is not surprising that people find hunting the sport of nabobs, but I have never understood the object of keeping twelve horses

[97]

when one third the number is amply sufficient. I know of cases where a dozen thoroughbreds are kept by one person in a two-days-a-week hunting country, and not a very hard one at that. This extravagance can be condoned in owners of the type that live with their horses, train, exercise and school them themselves — but, on the contrary, such stables generally belong to people who rarely look at their animals except when they are brought to the meet for them to ride, and the rest of the time leave them to the more or less capable and conscientious hands of grooms and strappers. Any horseman can understand the pleasure of owning as many horses as he possibly can if he dedicates all the time he can spare to them, and they constitute the great hobby and interest of his life, but when he can hardly tell one from the other, it is hard to understand what he gets out of them. The man who denies himself rather than give up his one beloved hunter is a type we would wish to see more of, for although he does not attract much notice at the meet and is rarely the central figure at hunt dinners, in the field he is generally not far from the "running houndes."

With "blood" go the highest qualities of stamina, pace and courage, but in a hunter we should never be so completely blinded by it as to neglect other traits which are quite as important.

[98]

There is a great and ever increasing taste in America for the thoroughbred hunter, a taste developed to such a degree that blood is frequently allowed to cover such sins as, for instance, lack of substance and bone. In my personal opinion the typical and best hunter is the well bred Irish type—and the old-fashioned stamp at that. Some thoroughbreds can indisputably give great satisfaction, but there are more "flat catchers" in the book than in twice the number of their humbler brethren. The average thoroughbred is apt to be a "pretty" horse — from which the Lord deliver us — showy and light of bone, especially below the knee — the antithesis of what a hunter, no matter what his weight, should really be, that is to say, an animal capable of hacking ten or twelve miles to the meet, carrying one well through a hard day, and hacking back at sun-down without distress in any weather — and doing this consistently three times a fortnight throughout the season, and for several November-to-March seasons.

Of course conditions vary in different countries and climates. In America, owing to motor traffic and macadam roads, it is the prevailing custom to van horses and hounds to and from meets, even the nearest to kennels; in Europe they generally hack both ways, and the return journey, even if tiring, is much more conducive to the health and good condition of horses

[99]

than a ride in a van after the heat and stress of the day, no matter how well blanketed they may be. When, furthermore, owners are in too much of a hurry to jump into their cars and go home to the hunt breakfast or cocktails to see that their mounts are properly cooled off before vanning, stiff shoulders and coughs next morning are the all too frequent result.

To return to the thoroughbred and the popularity he enjoys, particularly in the United States, I have heard it solemnly asserted that the pace in some American hunting countries is such that only the highest bred horses can live with hounds. I have not, unfortunately, had occasion to test the truth of this statement, but I can certainly say from personal experience — corroborated by the opinion of a well known American M.F.H.— that no pack whelped goes so fast that an ordinarily well bred hunter cannot keep up with it if ridden straight — and as the Irishman, provided he is up to his rider's weight, is quite as good a jumper, the size of the country is not sufficient reason either for preferring the thoroughbred. The same applies even to drags, which are supposed to be so very fast, if the riders really ride *to* hounds — that is *behind* them — and do not forget the pack altogether in the excitement of "riding jealous" and reaching the worry some few minutes before the leading hounds — as I believe has occasionally happened.

In England, drags are considered so little akin to actual hunting that they are not honoured with "pink," "rat-catcher" being the proper apparel for what is considered more of a "lark" than legitimate business. That drags can be both fast and stiff is obvious, but we are sometimes inclined to wonder why hounds are used at all; the runs could be faster and just as stiff without them, and as everyone knows beforehand where the line is laid and where it ends — generally in the vicinity of some hospitable mansion — the pageantry of pack, pink and hunt servants becomes almost an encumbrance and a spectacular superfluity — childishly dear to the hearts, however, of all sporting communities on both sides of the water except in England. The latter and Ireland are the only countries in the world where scarlet and Master's caps have their proper place and bear the right significance, and are not worn in and out of season even in the show ring; in this respect some of the worst offenders are on the European, not the American continent.

Drags would be more sporting propositions if they were at least always laid over a natural country; owing to the prevalence of wire, the "chicken coop" is inevitable in some parts, but "panelling" simplifies the line by all too evidently marking it and dispensing its followers from using their judgment as to where and how to jump their fences. Panels are bad enough when fitted into a natural fence or hedge, they are inexcusable when erected in the middle of an open field to be jumped over like the bars in a circus ring, and stupidly dangerous when placed on a front of a few feet, and of three different heights — for the good, the bad and the indifferent!

Hunting, like everything else worth doing, should be based on the survival of the fittest, and no good sportsman should wish for things to be made easy for him, as in the "pat" lawn tennis of the gay 'nineties when it was considered "rude" to hit a ball hard. If, for lack of heart, advancing years, or other reasons, we cannot face obstacles as we find them, let us be content to get our fun from the back of a cob through a pair of field glasses.

> *Still there's a path that a man can travel*
> *Happy at heart, though the roses die.*

PLATE 39

The forward seat

PLATE 40

Sport & General

The "Aintree" seat
Two styles of negotiating water

CHAPTER X

"I WAS never favourable to what is called steeple-chasing. In fact I have always looked upon it as the most cruel, the most unsportsmanlike, the most cocktail pursuit ever entered into by English gentlemen; more especially by real sportsmen. Each successive year has strengthened my opinion and now I am induced to speak up boldly, in consequence of what has just taken place at Liverpool, in a disgusting exhibition, absurdly designated the Great National Steeplechase. . . .

"In the first place its cruelty; we can have no right to call upon an animal to perform for us more than its natural powers enable him to do, without extreme danger to his life or at least great temporary suffering.

"Let us now look at the proceedings in the late Liverpool affair. Out of thirteen horses, first rate fencers, we may conclude with first rate horsemen on their backs, eight fell; clear proof that they were called upon to do what their mechanical construction disables them from doing. . . .

"First Cruikshank and Weathercock met in collision, the former falling against Weathercock, knocking off his rider, rolling upon him, etc. Next Hasty fell, and baulked The Sea, causing him to refuse . . . Then Valentine and Lottery race for the wall, when the latter fell. . . . Columbine, The Nun and Seventy-four next appear on their backs on the ground, with two of the three riders nearly killed.

"Here we have eight of the thirteen horses unable to keep on their legs, four of them falling opposite the Grand Stand before the ladies, the riders lying stunned and maimed before their eyes."

I have so far allowed the shade of Nimrod to "speak up boldly" for me, because, although the wall has long ago been done away with at Liverpool, the above lines, except for their humaneness, could have been written —where the actual description of the race is concerned —by any of the Aintree reporters of our day, who, however, are rather more inclined to wallow in such sadistic adjectives as "gruelling" and "lung-bursting" than to worry about the feelings of "the ladies."

Steeplechasing, born in Nimrod's day, raised the opposition of a large majority of his "real sportsmen" who were at that time all hunting men. Such progress, however, has been made, since *My Horses* was penned, in the breeding, "mechanical construction," schooling and training of the 'chaser that we no longer have to deplore, in other steeplechases, a tithe of the accidents that have, for ninety years, consistently marred the Liverpool "exhibition." Considering the intrinsically dangerous quality of the sport, serious mishaps elsewhere are remarkably few. Steeplechasing has taken a legitimate place in recognized sport, for, though practised over courses between flags, rails and wings, its relation to cross-country riding is still sufficiently close to absolve it from all impeachment of excessive artificiality, and *can* bring out all the best qualities of horsemen and sportsmen in those taking part in it. Nimrod himself would now agree, I think, and differentiate, as I do, between the "National"— and its fortunately rare counterparts — and other forms of steeplechasing.

Of late more than one voice has been raised in protest against a race that every year offers a spectacle which for casualties, among the horses at least, has little to envy the cavalry charges of Waterloo, Balaklava or Rézonville. The percentage of starters that pass the post at Aintree averages less than ten — a proportion difficult to explain either by the size of the fields or the length and severity of the course itself.

The size of the Aintree fences is indeed far in excess of anything one could possibly meet in a natural country; added to the distance (4½ miles) they constitute a formidable undertaking requiring the very best horses in the pink of condition, and at least courage of a high order on the part of the jockeys. Nevertheless I maintain that the National course would not in itself take a greater toll than other steeplechases were it ridden differently.

All variety in the Aintree course was done away with years ago with the suppression of the wall and, I believe, the bank and a certain amount of timber; and yet the world over no steeplechase course is complete without walls and some sort of timber (some courses in America are nothing but timber). The Auteuil course (Paris) has, besides, the "talus" and the "rail" of heavy solid wood, an "oxer" which would give food for thought if met with hunting, a natural brook over and above the water jump opposite the Grand Stand, etc.* In Italy a certain type of steeplechase—notably the Grande Steeple-chase di Roma — has an extraordinary variety of jumps, including timber in-and-outs; nevertheless none of these races give more than a reasonable percentage of falls and accidents, and the horses past the post are always far in excess of those left by the way. In all my very wide experience

* The "Grand Steeple-chase de Paris" is the same distance as the Grand National, i.e , 6,000 metres

PLATE 41

English steeplechase

PLATE 42

Italian steeplechase

PLATE 43 *Rotofotos*

Interesting study of inconsistency of position:
"Forward" on take-off, "backward" on landing

PLATE 44

Forward seat over high jump

I have never seen either death or "great temporary suffering" among the horses taking part in them.* We must therefore inevitably conclude that, where the "National" is concerned, "there is something rotten in the State" of Liverpool.

The fences at Aintree, with the exception of the water, Becher's and Valentine's, are all more or less of the same type — open ditches with very broad hedges, so broad and strong as even to permit tired horses to slide over them on their bellies if they can get their forehands over,† — a trick which would end in disaster over any other style of obstacle. It cannot even be argued that as neither walls, banks nor timber are typical of England, this steeplechase is characteristic of the English country, divided, as it generally is, by hedge and ditch. I do not think this reasoning, excellent though it may be for local point-to-point and hunt races, should apply to a purely conventional course such as Aintree. The bona fide hunter can per-

* Regarding danger to human life in steeplechasing as compared to other equestrian sports, figures of my own experience give paradoxical results I have personally known three men — one professional and two amateurs — killed racing over jumps, the first in a steeplechase, the last two in point-to-points Against these I can put five of my friends and acquaintances — all first-class horsemen — killed hacking, one by a horse coming down on him at a canter on the flat (on a race course!), another killed "larking" over a very small timber jump In thirty years' experience I have never seen anyone killed hunting, though I have seen half a dozen people badly, though not fatally, injured These statistics, oddly enough, would give hacking as the most dangerous exercise of the three, with steeplechasing second and hunting last!

† In this connection the photographs of "the second time around" are interesting.

haps be limited to jumps he is likely to encounter with his own particular hounds, but the steeplechaser, an entirely different stamp of animal kept as exclusively for the race course as the game cock was kept for the pit, should be capable of negotiating at racing pace any type of jump within reasonable size. Variety of jumps also requires better and more intelligent riding on the part of the jockeys. If at Liverpool, as at lesser English courses, all the jumps can be, and are, ridden at without differentiation, it is obvious that this cannot be done when tackling successively banks, oxers, open ditches, or a timber in-and-out.

It is currently stated that the size of the fences exacts the peculiar sit back kind of riding which delights our eyes at Aintree. This assertion belongs to the class of the many inconsidered ones we hear on all sides in matters of horsemanship, often from the mouths of people who should know better. What the size of the fences has to do with the matter it is difficult to understand, in the first place because it has now been proved for years that the forward seat is applicable to any angle a horse may make in jumping (see in particular Plate 44, which shows the rider sitting forward at the end of a jump 6 ft. 2 in. in height) and secondly because we see much the same type of seat in both professional and amateur English steeplechasing over jumps half the size of the Aintree fences (Plate 41).

The latter being high but also wide, it follows that the arc the horse describes in the air must be long and comparatively flat if he is to clear them at all — and nothing tends more to shorten the length of a horse's trajectory than weight on the loins and interference with his "balancier" at any stage of the jump. In the comments which accompany the press pictures of the Grand National a horse's fall on the landing side is frequently explained by the phrase "overjumped himself," whereas on the contrary he has jumped short, landed at too steep an angle and rolled over on his head and neck — a mishap all too evidently due, if we analyze it properly, to the sit back position of the rider and a pull on the mouth. We are told that when the horse is on the descending phase of the jump his rider frees his head by letting the reins slide through the fingers — what the French, who are credited with the invention, call *filer*. I will not here repeat what I have already gone into in the preceding pages to the effect that the horse should have his "balancier" free in all phases of the jump. It is too late to concede liberty of action half way over. On landing "à la Aintree" the jockey's hands are as far from the horse's mouth as the length of the reins will allow; but the jockey, having held on during the take-off, thanks to them entirely, and subsequently allowed his body to take from head to heel a position almost horizontal with his mount's

[109]

spine, the results are — what they are! Furthermore, having, after landing, regained a more or less normal position due only to the laws of gravity, he has to shorten his reins to regain control of his mount; before he is able to do this by bringing his hands forward by several consecutive movements, the horse enjoys full liberty at the very moment when he needs most steering; hence a large proportion of the "grief" by bumping and interfering of which the Canal Turn in particular offers outstanding examples. The horses, owing to the position with regard to the course of this particular fence, have to negotiate it sideways to the left; they land out of control, in complete disorder and are not put straight again for several strides. Is it surprising if under these conditions such a large proportion of the starters remain by the way or finish the course — for them happily — riderless?*

I think I may safely assume that having been so unbiased in all I have said in this book as to allow myself to criticise several nationalities not excluding my own,

* I understand that Mr. Victor Emanuel's entries, *Rhyticere* and *Royal Arch*, ridden "forward" by the French jockeys Nicudot and Bedeloup, finished fourth and eleventh in the Grand National of 1931, and that a species of forward seat was also adopted by Bob Lyall, the jockey of the winner, *Grackle* How forward or how correct Lyall's seat was I am not in a position to say; it has been described as *"vertical* from his seat to his head, with a *loose* rein," which does not sound reassuring, though it might constitute a step in the right direction Should we wish to go much farther back in the history of the National we could also mention the famous French steeplechase jockey Parfrement who rode the race "forward" in 1915 and repeated the performance on the same horse — *Lord Marcus* — the following year, finishing, without mishap, fifteenth and seventh respectively

—never in a narrow spirit of comparison, but whenever necessary to prove my points,— I cannot be accused of sycophantic tendencies if, writing for the American public, I say that American steeplechase and cross-country riders are superior to their British colleagues. Though their positions are not always perfect, they seem to have realized that forward riding is applicable to steeplechasing more than most amateurs or professionals outside of Italy or France. In my short experience of American point-to-points, hunt races or steeplechases, I have seen a much higher average of riding than in the American show ring, and rarely the disastrous interference with a horse's jumping powers so current in the British Isles. The photographs of steeplechases scattered through the pages of this book should be sufficient to convince anyone of the truth and impartiality of this statement. If, however, I may be allowed a closing remark, I would be inclined to say that American steeplechasing could be further improved upon if the riders kept in mind the position of the knee, which, I repeat with perhaps monotonous persistence, should *always* keep its place. Moreover, there is still a marked tendency to ride *forward* during the first phase of the jump — the easiest — and gradually *backwards* as the horse descends. Plate 43 is an extraordinarily instructive example of this. Taking the jockeys from left to right we see that the first three are properly forward, the fourth has thrust out his legs and is not only out of his saddle but *seated behind* it, and that the fifth has taken a position almost suggestive of Aintree — all of which leads one to suppose that they one and all began right but did not carry the correct position through, to the utter destruction of perpendiculars A-B and C-D of my chapter on "The Geometry of the Forward Seat."

As the sport that appeared on the horizon in Nimrod's day has become almost entirely professionalized, there is all the more reason for encouraging amateur point-to-points and hunt races.

Meticulous care should be taken to keep them within their true limits, to preserve their character of loyal gentlemen's pastimes, and promptly repress any tendency to apply to them either the mentality or the "tricks of the trade" of the professional environment.

A practice — for example — unworthy, strictly speaking, of the amateur milieu is the deliberate camouflaging of 'chasers into hunters — almost as unsporting a proceeding as palming off a professional jockey as a gentleman rider.

Slack "qualifying" on an occasional appearance at the meet and perhaps a canter or two of a few minutes after hounds, is responsible for our finding 'chasers in a type of race theoretically reserved to bona fide hunters. It is of course extremely difficult for a Mas-

ter — occupied as he is with his field and his hounds—
conscientiously to follow and observe the performance
of any individual horse out, but the result is serious,
for the entering of certain "hunters" in races in which
they have no business naturally discourages owners
of the real article, who find themselves outclassed and
retire before the invasion of horses which have no place
in anything but actual steeplechasing.

PLATE 45

Consistency of position in all phases of the jump
Tor di Quinto

PLATE 46

The forward position down hill
Tor di Quinto

CHAPTER XI

CONCLUSION

SUGGESTED to my mind by questions addressed me by American friends, this book has principally dealt with that part of the Italian method which concerns the seat (inevitable word!) and such accessories as have a direct bearing on it. I have tried to explain it to the best of my ability, and I hope my effort may contribute to clear the mists that in all countries outside of Italy — and especially in America — dim theories which have been so misunderstood as to sometimes leave even the most open minded either skeptical, puzzled or unconvinced.

If, in expounding the Italian seat, I may have seemed too uncompromising and constricting, this attitude has been deliberate on my part. There is no suggestion of relaxation in anything I have said under the heading "The Geometry of the Forward Seat." In no branch of knowledge do pupils need encouragement

[115]

to relax, and if the teaching itself lacks severity it fails to carry.

The Italian seat, moreover, is not learnt once for all, and its votaries will do well to keep this in mind. Like all things requiring accurate technique, continual practice is necessary not only to progress, but to prevent regress. Nothing, for example, is easier to lose than the proper position; especially in jumping, the heel may unconsciously go up or the body remain too erect or even swing back. The timely criticism of friends in schooling paddock or the open country should be welcomed by the best of us, for it makes one aware of imperfections which can easily escape one's own attention and result in slovenly and unaesthetic mannerisms.

This continual application may sound irksome to people inclined to believe that once having reached what they consider a fair average of horsemanship, there is no call for further effort — the same people who conscientiously strive every day to improve their golf, their tennis or their billiards! Horsemanship is not so much a pastime as a very difficult art.

From the purely technical I have been tempted to stray into other paths.

A typically Mediterranean *grand seigneur* indifference has caused my countrymen to suffer for years the free pirating of a system due to one of their race;

[116]

a sense of justice has induced me to put things in their proper place in my chapter on "Schools."

I have added my small voice to the chorus raised around certain controversial subjects which at the present moment are attracting considerable attention. I hope and think that what I say on the subject of certain forms of steeplechasing, from the angle of a method which above all considers the horse the gallant gentleman he is, will not seem idly iconoclastic.

I have also waged war against the false god of artificiality.

The day may come when in a crowded and mechanical world so little open country and so few wild animals will be left that hunting will be reduced to chasing the aniseed-bag, and any other form of riding restricted to rings — but it is not for us to hasten the dawn of that day. Men have tired of the race course, have grown, even after the most brilliant successes, sick to death of the show ring; no one has ever wearied of hunting, or renounced it with a light heart. "The best of my fun, I owe it to horse and hound." These are the words of a poet who died in the saddle — the hunting saddle.

As my book has been written with the great majority, and not the chosen few, in mind, I may perhaps be permitted to repeat what I have already said under another heading, namely, that although hunting is the noblest sport of all, it appeals to nobility of mind, not necessarily to that of purse. We are all equal in the hunting field, whether mounted on sons of Derby winners or on the sorriest of nags; the only difference that really matters lies in the purity of the flame that animates us, that *passione,* as we say in Italy, which makes us akin to the hunting gods of mythology when Reynard steals from cover and the first fence crosses our determined path.

Long after advancing years or the vicissitudes of human life have placed us *à pied,* and our saddles are nests for mice in some forgotten garret, the music of hounds will haunt our dreams. If for us then

> *... le son du cor*
> *Est triste au fond des bois*

with the sadness of things truly loved and irreparably lost, we shall still find sanctuary from the bitterness of vain regrets in the memory of spinney, and brook and plough, and the ever more distant echo of the galloping hoofs of braver and more thoughtless days.

Vale!